D0699933

*Slavery's End
in Tennessee,
1861–1865*

Slavery's End in Tennessee, 1861–1865

John Cimprich

THE UNIVERSITY OF ALABAMA PRESS

Library of Congress Cataloging in Publication Data

Cimprich, John, 1949–
    Slavery's end in Tennessee, 1861–1865.
    Bibliography: p.
    Includes index.
    1. Tennessee—History—Civil War, 1861–1865.
2. Slavery—Tennessee—Emancipation.   3. Afro-Americans—
Tennessee—History—19th century.   4. Tennessee—Race
relations.   I. Title.
E531.C56   1985   976.8′04′08996073   84-16200
ISBN 0-8173-0257-3

To my parents

Contents

Figures and Tables

Figures

Tables

Acknowledgments

This book began as a dissertation in 1974 under the guidance of Merton L. Dillon. He directed it with admirable skill, dedication, and patience through completion in 1977. During the years since then, his generous advice and encouragement have continued to aid my efforts. Other individuals whose critiques significantly improved the final product were Michael Les Benedict, Ira Berlin, Charles Eagles, Robert Ferris, Ralph Haskins, Vickie Hucker, Lester Lamon, Harriet Simon, and John Simon.

Research assistance was provided by Ken Heger, Sara Dunlap Jackson, Madeleine McKivigan, Bob Mainfort, and Joe Mannard. The work also greatly benefited from the services of hardworking staffs at a number of libraries and repositories, especially the National Archives, Ohio State University Library, Southeast Missouri State University Library, Tennessee State Library and Archives, and the University of Tennessee Library. Jack McKivigan gave valuable advice and encouragement throughout the years spent on this study.

A fellowship year, sponsored by the National Historical Publications and Records Commission at the Andrew Johnson Papers in 1979–80, stimulated fruitful rethinking of parts of the project. The Grants and Research Funding Committee, of the

Acknowledgments

Southeast Missouri State University, awarded generous financial support for the study's last stages.

I gratefully acknowledge permission to reprint material from "The Beginning of the Black Suffrage Movement in Tennessee, 1863–65," *Journal of Negro History*, LXV (Summer 1980), 185–95; "Military Governor Johnson and Tennessee Blacks, 1862–65," *Tennessee Historical Quarterly*, XXXIX (Winter 1980), 459–70; and "Slave Behavior during the Federal Occupation of Tennessee, 1862–1865," *Historian*, XLIV (May 1982), 335–46.

Finally, I would like to dedicate this book to my parents for teaching me the meaning of human dignity and much more as well.

John Cimprich
Cape Girardeau, Missouri

*Slavery's End
in Tennessee,
1861–1865*

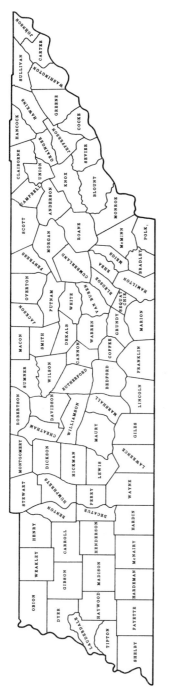

Figure 1. Tennessee Counties in 1861

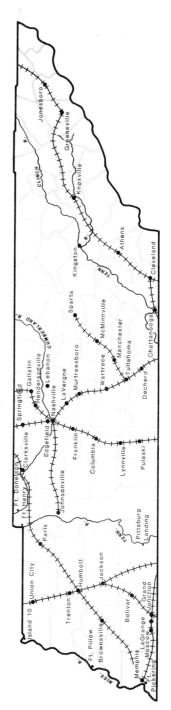

Figure 2. Key Towns and Railroads during the Civil War

Introduction

In the District of Columbia's Lincoln Park stands the national monument commemorating the emancipation of slaves during the Civil War. Financed by blacks but designed by whites, it depicts an erect Abraham Lincoln liberating a crouching slave. Although faithful enough to folklore, the symbolic bronze distorts the past by ignoring the internal forces that unraveled the "peculiar institution." Wherever federal armies operated, slaves took advantage of the conflict to declare themselves free. Their refusal to behave as slaves and their support of the Union cause put heavy pressure on the federal government for emancipation.[1] Although Lincoln played a major role, slaves should not be portrayed en masse as passive recipients of his benevolence.

Most historians today agree that numerous slaves asserted themselves during the war but disagree on why and to what extent. Some maintain that slaves manipulated the institution's paternalism for their personal gain but that in accommodating to it they became subtly inhibited by feelings of personal dependence and group weakness.[2] Others see slaves as independent-minded and deterred principally by the whites' physical power.[3] Each side defends itself from atop a pile of examples because no one can quantitatively analyze the psyches of several million long-deceased persons. A major difficulty in for-

3

mulating an interpretation is that the seemingly normal behavior of loyal* slaves provoked little contemporary comment. All of this study's evidence for a sense of dependency comes from a portion of those accounts, but none of it stands immune from alternate interpretations. On the other hand, much information exists about disloyal slaves and it supports the thesis of independent-mindedness. Therefore, while one part of the slave community remains relatively mysterious, the part that formed the cutting edge of emancipation will receive the primary attention here.

This book analyzes the roles—and more importantly the interaction—of slaves, masters, Federals, Confederates, Northern reformers, Southern unionists, and free blacks during the ending of slavery. A sense of personal worth impelled disloyal slaves to exploit the war-disrupted situation by seeking the privileges enjoyed by whites. Occasionally, masters had permitted slaves to exercise prerogatives technically beyond their status, such as education or private property. What the disloyal slaves wanted and won was the conversion of privileges for some blacks into rights for all. Free blacks actively aided the cause; federal officials and Northern reformers provided crucial, but limited, support. A minority of Southern whites, mostly unionists, gave up slavery under the stress of war; the majority struggled desperately to preserve it. The institution did not die quietly but screaming and clawing for survival.

In this drama, no individual black played a starring role in Tennessee; the story centers instead on the group. Because of the scarcity of literate slaves, historians possess much less information about the activities of blacks than about those of whites. Still, slaves clearly helped bring about social change. Although

---

*The words "loyal" and "disloyal" are not intended to connote value judgments in this book but merely to make a necessary distinction between slaves who did or did not take action against the institution.

freedmen remained at the bottom of the social system, their new privileges lifted the bottom from its former depths. The transformation of the status of an entire class constituted one of the most significant changes in the history of American society.

Tennessee lends itself to a case study of emancipation because of the length and extent of its federal occupation, a key disruptive factor during the war. The speed and manner of slavery's demise in the South varied with the strengths of the involved groups. In areas securely held by Confederates, the institution deteriorated less than in the zones of federal occupation. Louisiana and South Carolina, states with two of the largest percentages of slaves in their populations, experienced the most slave violence. The flight of all masters before federal occupation in the South Carolina Sea Islands hastened the breakdown of slavery there, while unionists' ability to retain civil governments retarded the process in the loyal border states. Despite local variations, emancipation remained basically the same social phenomenon throughout the South.[4]

1

The Institution
and the Confederates

Shortly before the 1861 referendum in Tennessee on separation from the Union, a slave sentenced to hang for killing an overseer spoke his last words from a gallows platform at Memphis. Isaac, the doomed man, argued that secession would do the South no good, that it would only make Southern white soldiers as guilty of murder as he was. Professing repentence, he urged secessionists to do likewise and thereby save the Union. Isaac's crime probably impressed white listeners more than his speech, for the preservation of slavery lay at the heart of the secession movement. In the words of two semiliterate Tennesseans: "The northern Abolitionast hav been steeling from the South and rasing inserectun in the south til the are determind to stand it no longer. . . . As we cant hav our property securd without it we are now determend to hav a confedracy of our own."[1]

They feared that, if anything undermined slavery, their entire way of life would be plunged into chaos. The 1860 presidential election of Abraham Lincoln precipitated fears into secession. Even though his Republican party officially advocated nothing more extreme than the prohibition of slavery's further expansion into Western territories, years of sectional conflict had heightened the South's sensitivity to criticism and caused many people there to believe that the Republicans really wanted abolition and racial equality. The survival of an institution that had profound economic and social significance seemed to be at stake.[2]

Slaves represented an important form of property, which, like all wealth, was unevenly distributed through Tennessee. Although about a third of the state's white families owned slaves, most masters possessed fewer than four, only 8 percent held more than twenty, and none had in excess of five hundred. Slaves composed 25 percent of the population but 34 percent of the value of taxable property just before the war. Many, possibly most, belonged to whites who owned ten or fewer bondsmen. The largest concentrations of slave property were in West and Middle Tennessee, the areas where commercial farming predominated (see figures 2 and 3).[3]

As a labor system, the institution provided much of the state's muscle. Agricultural slaves concentrated on the cultivation of cotton, tobacco, and corn, while industrial slaves labored mostly in the ironworks of northwestern Middle Tennessee. The remainder worked in transportation or domestic services. The system demanded respectful obedience and attention to the owners' interests. Slaves sometimes lightened their workload through deception, inveiglement, or overt resistance, but failure to fulfill duties could lead to physical punishment. Masters technically owed slaves only the provision of life-sustaining necessities; given the large numbers of owners and the vagaries of human nature, the treatment of slaves varied widely.[4]

Besides affecting the economy, slavery defined the bottom class in the social system. Few slaves—in 1860 only 174—rose into the state's miniscule free black class by manumission. Most blacks remained in a status that fixed their personal worth as negligible in terms of income and social privilege, a fact of major social significance. A secessionist mass meeting at Clarksville resolved: "Slavery is . . . of vital importance to the

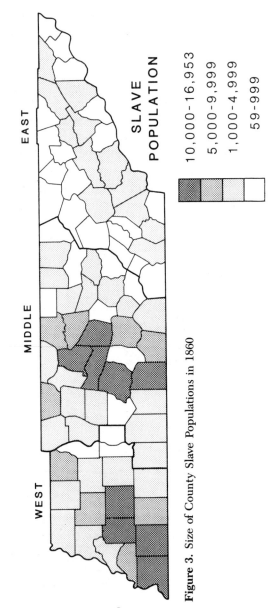

SLAVE
POPULATION

10,000-16,953

5,000-9,999

1,000-4,999

59-999

EAST

MIDDLE

WEST

Figure 3. Size of County Slave Populations in 1860

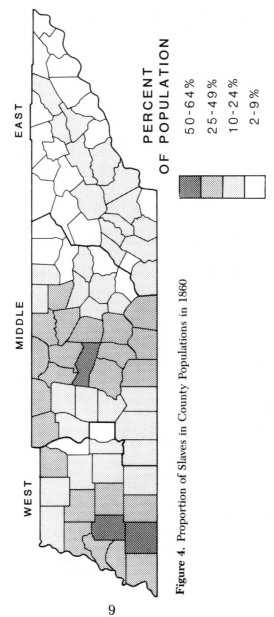

Figure 4. Proportion of Slaves in County Populations in 1860

PERCENT
OF POPULATION

50-64%
25-49%
10-24%
2-9%

EAST

MIDDLE

WEST

social and pecuniary interests of the Southern States, establishing as it does, the true *status* of the races, recognizing the social and political equality of the White men only, and allowing the degredation and vassalage only of the slave or inferior race."[5] Although secessionists' fears concentrated on an external threat to the institution, the war would reveal the extent of its internal instability, which required strong legal, physical, and social sanctions. Under Tennessee's prewar slave code, masters could use physical punishment almost without restriction. Slaves could not possess weapons without the county court's permission. They could consume liquor only with the owner's approval and only on his premises. To leave the property or to sell goods required a note written by the master. Slaves could congregate only when supervised by whites. Judges could sentence them to whipping, and no black could testify against whites in court. In Memphis, Nashville, and Columbia, local ordinances prohibited black education.

The codes also restricted whites. No master could permit slaves to hold a remunerative job or to act in any manner like a free person. Whites could not sell goods to a slave without the owner's permission. Interracial marriage was forbidden. The most serious offenses for whites were advocating abolition, aiding runaway slaves, and inciting insurrection. As with any law, the degree of enforcement varied from place to place and time to time, but during crises, such as the slave rebellion panic of 1856, heavy-handed enforcement by vigilantes and local authorities could occur.[6] As figure 3 shows, numerical superiority undergirded the physical power of whites in nearly all of Tennessee.

Social practices helped further to define and control the status of bondsmen. Whites expected submission from them while denying them important privileges. Showing little respect for the black family, masters separated 23 percent of a sample 1,291 West Tennessee couples through sale or relocation (see table 1).[7] Popular opinion usually prevented the education of slaves, though only a few municipalities prohibited it. An 1863 poll of 1,498 adult fugitives in Memphis revealed that only 2 percent could read.[8] Churches seated blacks in separate sections, and in some cases held services for them at a different time or in a different building. In a variety of ways, as one slave commented, "White folks they make us no 'count, . . . we's jes *slaves* and nuffin else."[9] The high degree of personal contact between master and slave, which was possible within Tennessee's numerous small slaveholdings, may have intensified the pressure upon slaves to accept their condition as fitting.

Table 1. Unbroken and Broken Unions of
Slave Couples from Three West Tennessee Counties

	Unbroken Unions	Broken Unions by Cause			
		Death	Master	Choice	Other
Percent	31%	33%	23%	7%	6%
Number	394	425	298	96	78

Nevertheless, their Christianity, their experience of abuse, and their observation of freedom's benefits worked against the system. Many prayed for freedom in secret religious meetings.[10] Some refused to accept punishment, resisted interference with their family, or covertly educated themselves. Within their own group, they could foster leadership and self-esteem. The institution's failure to make all slaves accept proslavery values incorporated a measure of instability into it.[11] As the legal, physical, and social sanctions broke down during the war, resistance would grow more open, elaborate, and effective.

During the secession crisis, all Tennessee politicians loudly proclaimed their commitment to slavery, but not all considered disunion a good means to safeguard it. Many Constitutional Unionists, led by William G. Brownlow, of the Knoxville *Whig*, and a splinter group of Democrats, headed by Senator Andrew Johnson, fought for the Union's preservation. They attracted significant support in several areas where the slave populations were small, especially East Tennessee. The unionists believed that a civil war provoked by secession would endanger slavery far more than Lincoln would. Realizing that the election results did not represent an abolitionist triumph, they contended that existing constitutional guarantees, reinforced by new political compromises, would ensure security for slavery. The outbreak of war in April 1861, however, ended all hope for compromise. In the subsequent referendum on Tennessee's separation from the Union, secessionists won 70 percent of the votes. The victors soon drove Brownlow, Johnson, and many of their followers from the state.[12]

Unable to tolerate internal opposition during the struggle for independence, secessionists warned Tennesseans to guard against unionist subversion and slave insurrection. Fearing both, all Confederate state legislatures established home guards. The Tennessee units were authorized to arrest suspicious persons, disarm slaves, break up their gatherings, and generally "keep the slave population in proper subjugation." In effect, they constituted legalized vigilante committees. According to small slaveholder George W. Matthews, the Maury County home guard hanged one slave for "incendiarism" and whipped "negroes supposed to be guilty" of burning corncribs.[13]

Numerous slave insurrection panics accompanied the secession crisis; at least five occurred in Tennessee during April and May 1861. The first two took place simultaneously in Lewisburg and Fayetteville after rumors circulated about the discovery of large-scale plots in neighboring counties. The Lewisburg *Southern Messenger* published an extra issue warning against rash acts of retribution, but these incidents seem to have ended quickly and quietly. The same outcome followed rumors of a nocturnal rebellion plot in Cleveland. Scares in Hawkins and Maury counties, though, resulted in the sentencing of three blacks to hanging. The fifth panic came after an early morning report in Jackson that slaves in a nearby hamlet had revolted. Later rumors claimed that militiamen were rushing from Memphis to save the town. By day's end, Jackson's inhabitants knew that an innocent party had caused the whole affair by firing a pistol several times.[14] Obviously, some Tennesseans felt very edgy.

Legislators who feared insurrection tried in late 1861 to stiffen the slave code. One bill proposed to make arson a capital crime for slaves, another would heavily fine masters whose bondsmen lived more than a mile from a white supervisor, and a third would prohibit manumission clauses in wills. The legislature rejected the arson bill, and federal invasion in early 1862 prevented voting on the other proposals.[15] No record of the debates exists to reveal why the arson measure was defeated; probably anxieties about slave rebellion had subsided.

Some whites never shared their neighbor's worries about uprisings. John Houston Bills, a halfhearted secessionist and large slaveholder in Hardeman County, grumbled that the home guard was a "wholly useless" and expensive operation. Another citizen reassured the governor: "The negro population were never so trusty. This illustrates his subordinate relation— he needs someone to cling to in the hour of peril." For most secessionists, it was probably the other way around; they could enjoy no peace of mind if they feared slave violence. Because proslavery theorists had argued that blacks were happiest as slaves and would refuse freedom if given a choice, a secessionist editor boasted: "Our slaves will be found loyal to their masters, and if necessary, we will arm such of them as we can spare from our fields to resist our foes, who will find in these pretended

13

objects of their philanthropy the ugliest customers they will have to encounter."[16]

Although the Confederate army never enlisted Tennessee's slaves, it used a select group as personal servants, most of whom remained loyal.[17] One officer's servant was annually sent home to help with the harvest, and he never took the opportunity to run away. Another slave fell into federal hands but chose to escape to his master. The faithful servants could have felt either a deep friendship for the master or a sense of paternalistic dependency; the evidence is unclear. The adventurous military life, though, could stimulate independent-mindedness, as when slaves stayed with the army after a soldiering master had died or been discharged. Under the law, they should have returned home.[18] Army experiences, then, could either reinforce or weaken servility.

Large numbers of slaves served as laborers for the Confederate army. Major Generals Gideon J. Pillow and Leonidas Polk called upon planters to volunteer hands to fortify Tennessee's Mississippi River border. John Houston Bills complained that the request was "a most villainous call, one he [Polk] has no right to make & is the beginning of a despotism worse than any European monarchy," but he grudgingly sent four slaves.[19] The generals received plenty of men until late 1861, when owners grew concerned about the dangers posed by hard work in winter weather. Confederate officials pressured slaveholders by setting quotas to be filled as a patriotic duty and by keeping "a list of those who refuse to aid their country's defense." The results were mixed: few owners refused outright, but many gave excuses for incomplete compliance.[20]

Construction of defenses along the Tennessee and Cumberland rivers slowed down for the same reason that winter. When offers of payment failed, commanders forcibly impressed the needed laborers, an act owners believed violated their rights. Some found means of eluding the military. After

Henry Yarbrough discovered that three of his four slaves were slated for impressment, he wrote: "I was a little too sharp for them. I called in Dr. Wilkerson, gave them some physic, and

Table 2. Average Slave Prices (Ages 12–40) behind
Confederate Lines in Tennessee, 1861–1863

Time Period		Sex	Recorded Prices (Number of slaves sold in parentheses)	Real Value (Charleston, S.C. rates)
1861:	Jan.–Mar.	M	$ 913.81 (41)	n.a.
		F	819.40 (25)	n.a.
	Apr.–June	M	1039.12 (17)	n.a.
		F	812.70 (10)	n.a.
	July–Sept.	M	924.73 (15)	n.a.
		F	847.70 (10)	n.a.
	Oct.–Dec.	M	943.41 (14)	$787.84
		F	772.06 (16)	643.31
	All 1861	M	944.94 (87)	n.a.
		F	810.52 (61)	n.a.
1862:	Jan.–Mar.	M	1091.94 (31)	909.95
		F	813.25 (10)	677.71
	Apr.–June	M	1055.00 (2)	703.33
		F	– – – – – – –	n.a.
	July–Sept.	M	– – – – – – –	n.a.
		F	– – – – – – –	n.a.
	Oct.–Dec.	M	1029.43 (14)	395.93
		F	1000.00 (1)	384.62
	All 1862	M	1071.75 (47)	n.a.
		F	830.23 (11)	n.a.
1863:	Jan.–Mar.	M	1480.00 (5)	451.42
		F	952.50 (5)	272.14
	Apr.–June	M	1800.00 (1)	321.43
		F	1400.00 (3)	250.00
	July–Aug.	M	– – – – – – –	n.a.
		F	2825.00 (4)	256.82
	Partial 1863	M	1533.33 (6)	n.a.
		F	1688.54 (12)	n.a.

then gave me a certificate [of exemption]. . . . There are some that begrudged us our negroes and would be glad they were all taken to the fort to die."[21]

After the federal invasion in early 1862, it became increasingly important to replace soldiers on noncombat details with hired or impressed slaves. The army offered to pay better than for usual slave hires, but the lack of cooperation continued. Most riverfront forts remained incomplete, weakening Tennessee's defenses against the enemy. One by one, Fort Henry, Fort Donelson, Clarksville, Nashville, Island No. 10, Fort Pillow, and Memphis fell. The authorities subsequently raised hiring rates even further, but spiraling inflation badly reduced lessors' real earnings. Popular pressure caused some regulation of impressment, most notably the rule that free blacks must be taken before slaves.[22]

Slaves shared the masters' opposition to impressment and usually disappeared if forewarned. One midwinter day, an individual named Granville failed to hide in time, and a patrol carried him off without allowing him to change into warmer clothing or obtain a blanket, lest he escape. Within three weeks, he fled home, but was in such ill health that death soon followed. The terrifying experience of combat prompted another impressed man to desert Fort Pillow for the comparative safety of his owner's plantation; he thought "a large ball of fire, nearly as big as the moon," had whizzed straight toward him during a federal bombardment in 1862. Rather than returning home, many runaways took advantage of proximity to federal lines to gain freedom. The loss of much slave manpower hurt Major General Braxton Bragg's army during the militarily crucial year of 1863.[23]

The Republican administration, which at first had banned military interference with slavery, began in 1862 to use abolition as a weapon. In July, Congress passed a measure that provided for the confiscation and liberation of slaves belonging to secessionists. Later in September, Lincoln's Preliminary

Emancipation Proclamation promised to free all slaves in the Confederate states, if the rebellion did not quickly end. Although the Final Emancipation Proclamation of January 1, 1863, exempted Tennessee, many federal authorities in the state showed little respect for the institution thereafter.

To impede the flight of slaves to the Federals, the Confederate Congress required its armies to capture those who were footloose, keep them in central locations, and publish their descriptions. In early 1863 a depot for captured fugitives was established at McMinnville, but Bragg soon moved it to Chattanooga to maintain a safer distance from federal lines and to facilitate use of the men in building fortifications.[24] The records contain no further mention of these captives after Chattanooga fell in the summer of 1863. A second depot, planned for Knoxville, seems never to have opened. Even though Confederate forces lost ground during the remainder of the conflict, their presence always deterred slave escapes. The two daily newspapers in East Tennessee, the region occupied longest by the Confederates, ran an average of only four new fugitive slave ads a month.[25]

The farther the distance behind Confederate lines in the state, the less slavery deteriorated.[26] In those areas, severe currency depreciation made the property value of slaves appear to increase, though their real value, determined by the gold conversion rate, probably declined sharply. That is the result when Charleston, South Carolina, rates are substituted for the unavailable Tennessee rates (see table 2). Had the Confederates won their independence, prices might have returned to prewar levels, as happened after the American Revolution.[27]

But the crusade for a proslavery nation failed. After the Confederates had lost most of the state, some desperate Tennesseans, including half the congressional delegation and several regimental commanders, called for the arming of slaves. Other whites bitterly opposed the idea as impractical and as a violation of Confederate principles. The slave recruitment law that

17

passed the Confederate Congress in 1865 came too late to be carried out in Tennessee.[28] In the spring of that year, the Confederacy expired.

Because Confederates fought to preserve a way of life built around slavery, the harm their armies directly inflicted on it in four years remained limited. Their retreat from areas where the slave populations were largest actually simplified the task of controlling slaves. Not until after the Federals occupied a locality did the institution begin to suffer severe damage.

2

The Master and Slave
Relationship
after Federal Occupation

Federal forces invaded Tennessee in February 1862 and occupied most of the state by late the next year. Shortly after Nashville's fall, a slave there discovered several soldiers pilfering his master's garden. Approaching one, he whispered a warning: "I'se gwine tar tell Marse Charles." The intruder stunned his adversary by replying "Damn your Marse Charles. What do I care?"[1] Everywhere the invaders established garrisons, slaves could observe their masters' seeming omnipotence gradually fizzle.

During this dramatic disruption, most owners struggled to preserve their interests in slavery, and some bondsmen asserted themselves against the institution in order to advance their interests. These basic facts have been clear to historians for several decades. The main point of debate is the issue of the slaves' motivation. One side argues that, though they wanted freedom and could have resisted, many refrained because of feelings of personal dependence and collective weakness stemming from their accommodation to paternalism; even those who were actively disloyal merely sought new rights within a revised paternalistic relationship.[2] The other side sees the slaves as being independent-minded enough to resist the subtle influences of paternalism. One version contends that a deep distrust of whites made them weigh the benefits and risks of

19

running away or staying before making a pragmatic decision; another holds that millennial expectations of freedom acted as disloyalty's driving force.[3] Evaluated in terms of the evidence from Tennessee, none of these interpretations can stand without qualification.

In at least their deportment, some slaves conformed to a paternalistic dependency. After Federals imprisoned the wealthy William G. Harding, Susanna, a domestic servant, wrote to her owner that none of his slaves had yet "disgraced" themselves by running off; nor did she think that any would leave unless "lured away with false hopes of equality and freedom." Susanna affirmed that their "true happiness consisted in doing their duty and remaining in their former condition." Of course, she may have mouthed such sentiments solely to curry favor with Harding. On the other hand, most of his 135 or so slaves remained on the plantation throughout the war despite its proximity to Nashville, a major refuge for runaways.[4]

Besides a paternalistic dependency, evidence suggests several other explanations for loyal behavior. Because Federals did not frequently appear in rural neighborhoods, isolation and routine could create loyalty by default: "We didn't know nothing else but slavery . . . never thought of nothing else. I just know I belonged to the man who provided for me and I had to take whatever he give me." Isolated slaves were more likely to believe propaganda depicting Federals as hostile to them. Others felt a genuine affection for owners. Still others acted upon a practical evaluation of their alternatives. After a thorough discussion, a group in Madison County decided that the "best thing to do was to be friendly & loyal & obedient to massas till freedom come."[5] Each of these mental states could exist without a sense of dependence.

The Federals' behavior affected the choices. The invaders frequently impressed blacks into work crews, driving them as hard and treating them as poorly as the Confederate army had.

Foraging expeditions at times took nearly all of a plantation's food supply; the troops also earned notoriety for theft, robbing even slaves of blankets, cooking utensils, and clothes. One family suffered the loss of their only treasured possessions: the husband's Sunday hat and pants, the wife's silk apron, and the daughter's party dress. Mischievousness, meanness, and racism motivated soldiers to perform cruel acts of abuse. For sport, a cavalry squad charged a field gang and ran them into a woods. The house slave Nancy became so afraid of Federals that she would work outdoors only when a child went along as a lookout. Other loyal slaves would certainly agree with her evaluation of them as "blue devils."[6] Indeed, such misbehavior convinced some slaves that the Union army was their enemy as well as that of their masters.

Yet, federal occupation also created opportunities for slaves to make choices. One factor behind adoption of resistance was the belief held by a portion of them that God had foreordained slavery's destruction in the near future because it suppressed blacks' rights. This conviction combined biblical imagery surrounding the Israelites' liberation from Egyptian slavery with millennial evangelism's sense of imminent divine action. The Civil War and the defeats suffered by the Confederates provided an apocalyptic setting for the expected providential deliverance of slaves and punishment of masters. When a federal troop carrier steamed up the Cumberland in early 1862, the passengers saw about fifty blacks dancing on shore and singing:

> O, praise and tanks! de Lord he come
> To set de people free
> An, massa tink it day of doom
> An' we of Jubilee.

As federal cavalry entered Nashville shortly after its fall, slaves lined the streets shouting "Bress de Lord! Moses am a comin to deliber Isrel from bondage! Glory Hallelujah!"[7] These people envisioned not a millennial era of human perfection but only a new and better day for their race. Still, the war transformed the doctrine of deliverance from a comforting belief to a driving force behind a vanguard's efforts to change the status of slaves.[8]

Not all of them held or were motivated by a belief in their deliverance. Some acted disloyally only after coolly calculating the probabilities of their immediate benefit. Aleck, a runaway from Haywood County, expressed a rule of thumb for fellow slaves: "if they have good homes that they had better stay where they are . . . if they run off they have no homes, and perhaps can't get any work," but, if their masters were cruel or their subsistence poor, they had everything to gain and nothing to lose by leaving.[9]

Circumstances early in the war often seemed to stack the odds in favor of disloyalty. By chance or by stealth, many slaves heard owners repeat the Confederate charge that the North wanted to free slaves and subjugate white Southerners. Slaves could see that extensive enlistments (eventually exceeding 80 percent of white males who had been fifteen years of age or older in 1860) either ended or sharply reduced the white majority in most of rural Tennessee. Some bondsmen found themselves abandoned by masters who hastily fled the advancing Federals.[10] They watched as local government gradually lost its ability to discipline them during federal occupation.

Desiring freedom and aware of their masters' weakness, many slaves who lived near federal garrisons abandoned their respectful demeanor and servile obedience. Like many other slaveholders, Robert H. Cartmell, of Madison County, reacted bitterly: "To one born and raised in the South & accustomed to keeping the Sons of Ham in their proper place, the impudence of these negroes is hard to endure. They are entirely corrupted."[11]

Disloyal slaves applied peer pressure on their associates. On

Rebecca Ridley's Rutherford County farm, "We have three that are perfectly faithful I think, & yet they are unhappy." One of the loyal individuals began to drink openly and heavily as his relations with the dissidents grew more strained. Cartmell's slave Easter alone continued to serve his family until a harsh comment from his wife caused her to walk out of the kitchen forever. That night, a number of blacks met at Easter's cabin to celebrate her conversion.[12] Disloyalty could grow slowly, but it spread contagiously to all who lacked the immunity of adamant loyalty.

Disloyal slaves secretly assisted the federal army by reporting information about their owners and the Confederates. In one scout's opinion, "they seem to know evry [*sic*] thing and are pretty shrewd too," but, like any intelligence source, they also provided insignificant and inaccurate data. The informants helped mostly by reporting Confederate movements and the location of hidden supplies.[13] Officers encouraged these slaves by offering them protection or rewards because of the dangers involved in betraying the secessionist owners' cause.[14]

The most visible expression of disloyalty was running away. Most of the first runaways after the federal invasion were males between the ages of sixteen and thirty-five, the same group that predominated in prewar escape attempts. They constituted approximately 70 percent both of the captured fugitives advertised by the Davidson County jail after the city's fall and of the advertised runaways from East Tennessee while it remained under Confederate control. In time, the stream of runaways grew more varied. In early 1863 Memphis camps for the contrabands (the army's designation for fugitive slaves) contained 52 percent children, 25 percent adult females, and 23 percent adult males.[15]

The boldest and most hopeful slaves fled soon after Federals entered the neighborhood. Others tarried until anger, fear, need, force, or certainty of freedom impelled them to act.

Attempts to discipline slaves became counterproductive, especially if federal troops in the locality accepted fugitives in camp. Just after the Union army occupied Williamson County, an elderly slaveholder tried to whip a teenage slave for poor work. The youth threw the old man to the ground, armed himself with an ax, and walked off the farm. Even the threat of punishment could cause flight because opportunity for escape sharply reduced tolerance for slavery's harsher aspects.[16]

Some individuals ran away only when they came to fear that Southern whites would regain dominance over them or their loved ones. One woman fled with her children the night after she discovered that their master intended to send the youngsters through Confederate lines for sale. Federal withdrawal from an area frequently touched off a mass exodus of slaves. Fugitives feared that the advancing Confederates would impress them, remove them to the Deep South, or even execute them. Having rejected slavery, they both dreaded and detested the forces of the Confederacy.[17]

Slaves left in some cases because of federal interference. Although commanders initially prohibited it, Union soldiers occasionally liberated slaves to punish avowed secessionists. Cautious slaves took full advantage of this situation; the contraband George Knox explained: "If I were captured and taken away by the Yankees, and not satisfied, I could come back and the rebels have nothing against me." A more harrowing circumstance was the appropriation by Federals of so much of a farm's food supply that the slaves needed to desert their owner in order to find a new source of subsistence.[18] The occupying power could easily wreak havoc upon slavery if it so chose. Interference, rare at first, increased as the war dragged on and the army dropped its restrictions.

Whatever the immediate reason for departure, runaways felt a fundamental attraction to freedom. This desire could supersede friendship for a master, material comforts, and even memories of mistreatment at federal hands. The boy Joel told the mistress who wanted him to come back: "I intend to stay and go to school & be free . . . goodbye—don't you ever come back here for me." When a Federal advised an elderly contraband to return home because the soldier doubted that he could survive by himself, "the old man replied that if he lived only one day . . . he would live that day a free man."[19]

Fugitives did not always find satisfaction in freedom. Hardship or homesickness could bring them back. After miserable experiences in an independent life, some longed for a paternalistic master. The returned runaway John influenced his fellows to stay home and wept uncontrollably when Federals impressed him. Others remained discontented, like Cherry, who refused to behave in servile fashion, argued with her owner, and ran away repeatedly only to come back later. Unless a returned slave behaved submissively, the master-slave relationship grew more strained.[20]

Slaves sometimes chose not to flee the institution but to subvert it. Spending their time however and wherever they wished, they refused to obey commands or to accept punishment. Some lived only for self-gratification at their owners' expense; others sought to end the slave labor system by holding what amounted to a strike, using for leverage idleness, the threat of running away, and occasionally an incriminating knowledge of a master's pro-Confederate activities.[21] Primarily these slaves wanted compensation in the form of wages, a share of the crop, or the use of land for growing their own market crops. Some also demanded a shorter workweek or the elimination of overseer supervision. A labor shortage, caused by the runaways, aided the negotiating position of those who remained in rural areas.[22]

Bargaining slaves showed a sense of collective strength. Acting as a group to substitute a contractual relationship for a paternalistic one, they upset masters far more than did runaways. Resolute slaveholders, like Robert H. Cartmell, refused to make any concessions. In his case, all the slaves but one eventually left him rather than capitulate. John Houston Bills tried to do as Cartmell did but could not persevere. Bills assigned to federal impressment the first slave who refused to work, but a year later, when he threatened to do the same to another idler, she retorted that she would jump off his wagon and run back to the plantation. Realizing that "we have not the power to control them," Bills and a number of other planters acceded to the demands in order to keep their farming operations from coming to a halt, as Cartmell's had. When the hands on one of Bills's plantations produced only thirteen small bales of cotton for him and six large ones for themselves, the master, ironically enough, felt exploited: "Matters truly discouraging—negro slavery of no value, but much expense."[23]

Resistance in the form of violence was rare, for slaves could assert themselves in a variety of more effective ways that involved fewer deterrents and dangers. The presence of informants in the slave community worked against successful conspiracy. Lack of military training and restrictions on the possession of guns further complicated revolutionary activity. By all indications, Federals, like Confederates, would have mercilessly crushed a slave uprising. Tennessee blacks knew about these difficulties. As one slave told a unionist scout, "Dis dark'y tinks a heap ob his life, he does, Massa. It'm 'bout all hem got. . . . No, I hain't no coward, Massa; but I loikes a chance, Massa, a right smart chance."[24] Slaves normally relied on stealth rather than on violence to gain freedom; only a few tried to kill their owners in acts of personal revenge.[25] Most of those who were willing to use violence did so by enlisting in the federal army once that became possible in 1863.

Slave disloyalty in any of its wartime forms challenged proslavery ideology, which portrayed the institution as necessary and beneficent. Bills could not comprehend "the very strange

26

infatuation" that impelled some of his charges to seek freedom at the cost of their material comfort. It seemed impossible to Henry Craft, of Memphis, that an institution supposedly ordained by God could ever end: "a very large number of the negroes will not accept their freedom & . . . by one name or another, pretty much the old relations will be established." Yet, current events caused doubts. Craft worried that "if we adopt the theory that God intended the war to free the slaves, all the phenomena of the war harmonize and fall in with it most wonderfully."[26]

A small number of slaveholders, mostly unionists, underwent a change of heart and began compensating their slaves before any signs of disloyalty appeared. In 1864 Joseph B. Killebrew, of Montgomery County, started paying a generous annual wage of $200 for men and $96–$120 for women, plus room and board for all. A Shelby County planter offered his slaves half the crop that year. James P. Lyon had gone even further the year before by dividing his Madison County plantation into tenant farms for his slaves. Reminiscing later, Killebrew concluded: "I got along with my hands much better than I expected."[27]

Most masters remained firmly committed to slavery, blaming all their troubles on Northern agitation. In an effort to retain control, they tried to poison the blacks' minds against the Federals. Sometimes they portrayed the enemy as monsters. Twelve-year-old Betty learned from her mistress that Federals possessed horns, long canine teeth, and cow-like eyes. Because Betty affectionately served as nurse for the two babies of the mistress, the latter added that the Federals would kill the babies upon learning that they had been named Sterling Price and Susie Beauregard in honor of Confederate generals. One day during the absence of the mistress a passerby questioned Betty about the farm and its owners. Inasmuch as his appearance did not match her image of a Federal, she answered his queries, including one about the children's names. The stranger later returned with blue-clad soldiers to sack the farm. If nothing more, the "monster" stories hurt the teller's credibility when the real Federals arrived.[28]

Propaganda could take more plausible forms. Masters insisted that the Federals would cruelly overwork captured slaves, a claim made credible by the experiences of those impressed for labor gangs. All across the South, slaveholders characterized as standard practice an exceptional incident in which a federal officer on a South Carolina Sea Island attempted to ship contrabands to Cuba for sale. Owners constantly warned bondsmen that Northerners meant to harm all Southerners regardless of race, but the allegations did not sway everyone. Once the Federals arrived, some felt like the slave who said: "I thought you must be downright heathens, but you are real good-looking people and don't seem to do nobody harm."[29]

As the Federal government gradually moved toward emancipation, masters who discussed the matter with slaves usually claimed that the invaders intended not to free but to exploit them. William B. Lewis, a Nashville unionist, showed greater subtlety by advising his wards to stay at home until the government made a final decision on their legal status and pointing out that the whites would punish runaways with a vengeance if emancipation did not occur. Persuasive efforts met with partial success but hardly stopped the flow of fugitives through federal lines.[30]

Other owners considered silence a wiser strategy. Sarah Kennedy, of Clarksville, tried to avoid trouble with her slaves by showing no sign that she was "looking for any excitement." Despite such efforts, news of the proclamation spread through parts of the slave community. Tennessee's exemption from the Final Emancipation Proclamation must have come as a disappointment, but informed slaves would have realized that the federal government had openly turned against slavery.[31]

Besides playing upon ignorance and purveying misinformation, masters used paternalism as a psychological weapon. The canny William B. Lewis advised a friend to "look closely after those who are still at home and direct your overseers to abstain, as far as possible, from giving them any excuse for leaving you." White preachers exhorted slaves to respond to paternal care with faithful service and prayers for the Confederate cause. In an emotional meeting, Ebenezer Johnson, of Loudon County, and his last slave, Henry, reaffirmed their mutual obligations. Henry's wife, a runaway, had almost talked her husband into leaving, but either a sense of duty or cautiousness kept him with Johnson. Other slaves performed the rituals required by the system, then prayed in secret religious meetings for the Federals' success and slavery's end.[32]

In addition to psychological tactics, slaveholders resorted to physical force. The most effective method was to move their wards as far as possible behind Confederate lines. Taken deep into the state's mountainous northeast, the slave Wiley heard nothing more about the war until it ended. This method required vigilance and raw power, lest bondsmen take alarm and escape.[33]

Masters occasionally tried to halt the spread of disloyalty by selling the most troublesome slaves. Although federal commanders never prohibited slave sales, popular opinion in Tennessee held that the allegedly abolitionist Northerners would severely punish the sellers.[34] Sales tended to occur covertly; the deed books of occupied counties record only a few purchases at low prices.[35]

Slaveholders who intended neither to sell nor move their chattels often resorted to other forms of control by force. Children could simply be locked in the house, but no easy method existed for preventing the flight of adults. Owners recovered some runaways through dogged pursuit or clandestine kidnapping.[36] Recaptured slaves usually received a severe whipping,

29

and a few were killed. One master kept an obstinate runaway confined for eight weeks on a starvation diet, which so weakened him that he could never make another attempt to escape.[37]

Owners increased their strength through vigilante action, a traditional method for handling slavery's crises. In at least Coffee, Hickman, Maury, Montgomery, Shelby, and Warren counties, civilian bands and Confederate guerrillas employed violence and terror in efforts to maintain slavery behind federal lines. These organizations patrolled rural neighborhoods, just as home guards did under the Confederate government.[38]

Yet, masters who used force against recalcitrant slaves needed to take care not to antagonize the Federals. Open brutality could cause military intervention by activating sympathy for a victim, hostility toward secessionists, or concern for civil order. Manson M. Brien, a prominent Nashville unionist, nearly caused a riot in 1863 when he seized a fugitive slave as she left a black church service. A passing provost guard calmed a mob of outraged blacks by arresting Brien, though they subsequently released him with a warning. During 1863–65 incidents occurred all across the state in which soldiers prevented masters from whipping or recapturing slaves.[39]

Despite the tactics that slaveholders used, nothing could ensure that bondsmen would remain loyal during federal occupation. Sometimes master and slave retained affection for each other after the relationship was severed. A few masters sent runaways friendly messages and gifts; some contrabands enjoyed visiting owners and made it clear, as a black soldier put it, "I ain't fighting you, I'm fighting to get free."[40] More often, disloyalty sliced a cold chasm down the middle of the relationship. When the slaves of Episcopal Bishop James H. Otey ran away, they took half his furniture and clothing. Offended by "the destructive views into which their new-born liberty would lead them," he felt little sorrow or sympathy, except for the black children, when the disloyal ones left. Some disillusioned slaveholders even drove unfaithful servants from the premises.[41]

While masters might consider disloyal slaves as traitors and ingrates, the slaves might view their masters as exploiters and abusers. When Federals liberated the blacks on a Fayette County plantation, an elderly female scolded her owner in the soldiers' presence for mistreatment of his slaves. Robert H. Cartmell spoke for the angriest slaveholders: "This war has demonstrated one fact: That the negroes *generally* would betray their masters when an opportunity presented itself." He tried to insulate himself emotionally and physically from his slaves' disloyalty: "I never go about them, . . . shall have nothing to do with any of them as long as I can not control them."[42]

Federal occupation created a situation that damaged slavery structurally by interfering with the owners' ability to manage and care for their slaves, in other words to carry out their role as masters. Paternalism, pragmatism, isolation, or affection kept some slaves loyal. Visionary hopes or pragmatism motivated others to attempt an improvement in their status. The resisting

Table 3. Available Numerical Data
on Tennessee Contrabands, 1865

Blacks in contraband camps (July 1, 1865)		7,151
Black civilians not in contraband camps:		
Memphis (August 18, 1865)		15,828
Nashville (August 10, 1865)		10,744
Chattanooga (November 6, 1865)		2,657
	Subtotal	29,229
Black Enlistees (April 1863–June 1865)		20,133
	Grand Total	56,513

31

blacks' refusal to fulfill their role as slaves added another dimension to the social conflict of the Civil War. Because this group actively supported the Federals, the occupying army rarely interfered with the disloyalty and gradually came to encourage it. Thinking in proslavery absolutes, most masters could only respond with moral indignation and disgust toward the disloyal slaves and the Federals.

One manifestation of disloyalty, flight from the master, can be measured to a degree because the Federals kept records for some but not all contrabands. Table 3 shows that disloyalty affected at least a significant minority. The table's grand total would represent about 20 percent of the state's slaves except that it includes an uncertain number from neighboring states and from the free black community.[43] Even if disloyal slaves were exceptions to the rule, they were the ones who caused new rules to be made.

3

Federal Occupation
and the Slave Code

On March 13, 1862, Andrew Johnson returned to Tennessee as a brigadier general and military governor. Soon after his arrival in Nashville, he issued an "Appeal to the People of Tennessee" that accused the Confederates of destroying state government and rule by law. He pledged to restore both and, in addition, to uphold citizens' legal rights; the latter implied that he would safeguard slaveholders' property rights. He did not yet comprehend the problem of preserving rights in the midst of civil war. Constant offers of service from fugitive slaves tempted Federals not to sustain the property rights of masters, most of whom still supported the Confederacy. Proslavery ideals had limited Confederate infringements upon the institution, but a conquering enemy need not respect anything except what it chose to respect. As the slave Susanna perceived, "Law and order are at an end and the law of might is now the rule by which all govern themselves."[1]

Power in the occupation zone lay mostly in the federal army's hands. Both President Lincoln and Congress at first disavowed any intention of using military force to harm slavery, but in the war's second month several slaves had challenged the government's position by seeking refuge at a federal fort in Virginia. The War Department subsequently ruled that commanders could accept fugitive slaves when they deemed it militarily necessary. Although the status of runaways as property would remain unchanged, the legal problem of their disposition would be postponed until after the war. Thus, the high command exploited slave disloyalty but remained reluctant to tamper with the institution. Fugitives soon gained the nickname of "contrabands," short for "contraband of war."[2]

By the time Johnson issued his "Appeal," Congress had modified its stand on the slavery issue with two important laws. The First Confiscation Act allowed the army to confiscate slaves used as military laborers by Confederates but did not explicitly free them. A new article of war prohibited federal troops from returning fugitive slaves, lest secessionists profit.[3] Military expediency and a shift toward emancipation by the radical wing of the Republican party began to pry the government away from its original policy of preserving slavery inviolate.

Congress and the War Department set only the general parameters of policy for runaway slaves; field commanders were forced to devise specific applications with little guidance. The first federal commanders in Tennessee viewed interference with slavery as militarily and politically unwise. "If runaway negroes are encouraged we will soon be overwhelmed with them," a staff officer wrote. "They would soon eat us out, encumber our march & give ground for the assertion that we came South to steal negroes." If federal officers could dispel Southern fears that their government wanted abolition, they believed the war would end soon.[4] The military units that invaded Tennessee in February 1862 maintained similar policies for fugitive slaves. Major General Henry W. Halleck, when sending Major General Ulysses S. Grant to attack Forts Henry and Donelson, ordered the exclusion of runaways from federal lines. The navy's riverboat fleet prohibited slaves from coming aboard ship. Major General Don Carlos Buell, whose army occupied Nashville, not only excluded fugitive slaves but also allowed masters to search for and recapture those who had penetrated his lines.[5] Technically, these policies did not violate the new article of war because soldiers did not directly return runaways, yet the institution of slavery certainly received indirect support.

Through the summer of 1862, slaves could find few Federals who would disobey the exclusion orders. Outside the army camps, runaways encountered much difficulty in finding secure hiding places because newspapers still carried advertisements for fugitive slaves and municipal police energetically searched for them. The safety of contrabands lay mostly in their increasing numbers.[6]

Small breaches soon appeared in the federal policy. When Fort Donelson fell, Grant used the First Confiscation Act to sequester the construction gang slaves. Officers' servants, whom he did not consider to be military laborers, accompanied their masters to prison. Viewing the confiscated slaves as property, he used them in military support capacities. Other officers followed his example as the occupation spread.[7] In April 1862 both Buell and Halleck exempted from exclusion the slaves who reported military intelligence. Grant stretched the new order to include even those who related useless information. By June the need for laborers led to the impressment of black males, some of whom actually sought it to escape slavery. Thus, military needs and the willingness of contrabands to serve were undermining the exclusion policy.[8]

Federals who held antislavery convictions chafed under the policy from the start. Colonel John Beatty, of the 3d Ohio Infantry, detested slavery and at first readily permitted fugitives to remain in his camp. In his opinion, "If a dog came up wagging his tail at sight of us, we could not help liking him better than the master, who not only looks sullen and cross at our approach but in his heart desires our destruction." Under Buell's orders, Beatty's brigade once had to march contrabands out of camp. When the colonel learned that fugitive slave hunters knew the time and place of the operation, he forewarned the blacks, who disappeared in time.[9]

Other Federals never doubted the propriety of slavery until wartime experience changed their minds. One such man, Private Elisha Stockwell, while walking through the woods at Pittsburg Landing, chanced upon a white man holding a black at gunpoint and claiming he had run away from a neighbor. Knowing his orders, the soldier told the slave that the Federals could neither admit slaves into camp nor interfere with the institution. A troubled Stockwell watched as the fugitive was bound and led away. The sight of slavery's uglier aspects, such as hunts for fugitives, auctions, near-white mulatto slaves, and whippings, could shock Northerners out of complacency.[10]

Some Federals never modified their prejudices but came to detest the exclusion policy through their hostility toward secessionists. The 7th Pennsylvania Cavalry stopped allowing slave hunters in camp after one group, which carelessly opened fire on a contraband fleeing through the tent site, turned out to be Confederates. The hatred many Federals felt for their enemy intensified as hope for a short war dissipated. A soldier who considered blacks suitable only for slavery could still write: "I have no trouble in believing that all these rebels should loose every slave they possess; and I experience some pleasure in taking them [the slaves] when ordered to."[11]

Increasingly unpopular with the troops and under fire from radical Republicans, the exclusion policy crumbled. The process moved most rapidly in West Tennessee, where opponents made little effort to keep runaways out of the camps and claimed that the new article of war prohibited their expulsion. A major confrontation occurred in June 1862, when Lieutenant Colonel Daniel Anthony, 7th Kansas Cavalry, refused to expel several slaves in the presence of their master. Halleck had Anthony arrested and used a surprise search to recover some of the slaves. Soon afterward, fearing that the case would stir up a political hornet's nest, Halleck had Anthony released.[12]

Two events brought an end to the policy in West Tennessee: the passage of the Second Confiscation Act and Halleck's promotion to general-in-chief. Passed in July 1862, the act confiscated and freed secessionists' slaves who came within federal lines. Although the law took a big step toward general emancipation, it neither explicitly banned exclusion policies nor designated authorities, outside of courts, to declare eligible slaves free. Also during July, Halleck's promotion took him to a more politically sensitive job in Washington and allowed Grant to assume a command that was soon designated as the Department of the Tennessee. Grant, now convinced that the Confederate cause would suffer from federal use of slave manpower, said nothing about the exclusion policy left behind by Halleck.[13] In the absense of directions, some subordinates persisted in excluding contrabands, while others stopped in the belief that it violated the spirit of the Second Confiscation Act. In November, Grant finally requested and obtained Halleck's permission to accept, protect, and use contrabands without restriction. The navy's upper Mississippi River fleet had already dropped the exclusion policy during September in order to gain needed laborers.[14]

The army's interference with slavery caused friction with civil governments. Once the Federals accepted and employed contrabands, Memphis police no longer dared to arrest them. The city's unionist leaders turned to the federal circuit court to obtain the appointment of a federal fugitive slave commissioner, who under the Fugitive Slave Act of 1850 could order runaways returned. The post commander then ended the matter by suspending the slave code. In Nashville, the unionist city government could not cope with the flood of runaways and sought help from Major General William S. Rosecrans, who had replaced Buell and assumed command of a new Department of the Cumberland. Protesting that local law enforcement was not his responsibility, he refused the request of the officials either to expel contrabands from the city or to place them under military supervision. His need for laborers led by early 1863 to an order allowing all able-bodied black men through the lines for the sole purpose of military employment. Several policemen secretly captured and returned runaways for a fee until exposed by an army investigation. After one year, federal occupation had rendered local civil government totally ineffective in controlling slave flight. When hopes for a short war were shattered by early 1863, all top federal commanders in the state had decided to use slaves in a heightened war effort.[15]

Rosecrans, however, prohibited women, children, and unemployable men from entering his lines. His subordinates tried to follow orders, but as one soldier remembered: "They could not be kept out, for they came in spite of orders. . . . When they came our officers could no more find it in their hearts to drive the poor things away than mother or father could drive children forth from their home into a driving storm."

The increasing flood of contrabands continued to force the issue, and several Middle Tennessee post commanders quietly stopped trying to separate black laborers from their families. After opening his post to all contrabands, the commander of Fort Donelson bluntly reported to department headquarters his total frustration with the rules. Rosecrans replied with an order that reaffirmed his partial exclusion policy, but, because of prodding from the War Department, permitted exceptions in "cases where humanity demands it."[16]

In the fall of 1863 Major General George H. Thomas replaced Rosecrans. A Southern nationalist who possessed strong racial biases and whose wife was a slaveholder, he ignored the War Department's preferences and ordered all contraband women and children excluded from his lines. By this time, many of his subordinates had embraced emancipation. Brigadier General Grenville M. Dodge, for example, had stopped excluding contrabands from his post at Pulaski on the grounds that "every officer and Loyal man should do his best to put an end to the evil that has caused this war and that keeps you and me a thousand miles from our homes."[17] Such officers would not have easily accepted the restoration of a partial exclusion policy. They never needed to because Brigadier General Lorenzo Thomas, adjutant general of the national forces, intervened.

Although once a slave owner, Adjutant General Thomas evolved during the war into a staunch emancipationist, boasting in an 1863 speech: "I know what all the prejudices are upon that subject but I have overcome them." He played a central role in contraband affairs in the Mississippi Valley after Secretary of War Edwin M. Stanton assigned him to supervise contraband recruiting and labor programs there. Although the adjutant general viewed contrabands primarily as an exploitable resource, he also exhibited some humanitarian concern for their welfare. The day after General George H. Thomas revived the partial exclusion policy, the adjutant general nullified it by establishing a refugee camp within the Department of the Cumberland for fugitive slaves of all ages and both sexes.[18]

The army now officially encouraged contrabands, but some Federals continued to use military might to uphold slavery. Particularly in rural areas, where they did not attract their superiors' attention, officers ordered slaves to stay home and returned runaways in violation of the Articles of War.[19] A major controversy arose over the fugitive slave policies of Major General Lovell H. Rousseau, a Kentuckian who commanded the District of Middle Tennessee.[20] Shortly after Adjutant General Thomas founded the contraband camp for the Department of the Cumberland, Rousseau tried to exclude juvenile and elderly contrabands from nearby federal lines. The order was soon forgotten, but not before winning him the enmity of Colonel Reuben D. Mussey, an Ohio abolitionist who directed black recruiting in Middle Tennessee. Mussey began a vindictive campaign for Rousseau's dismissal by ferreting out the general's written permission for a Kentucky unionist to regain a runaway slave by force. The colonel then collected witnesses who claimed to know of similar orders and reported his evidence to two special investigators whom the War Department appointed.[21] Rousseau refused to cooperate with the inquiry; moreover, he disbanded a court-martial then trying the Columbia post commander for violating the Articles of War regarding fugitive slaves. The investigation, though critical of the general, did not result in his removal, probably because he was politically influential, he did not use troops to return runaways, and the unionists retained a legal right to slave property.[22]

Although by 1863 few federal officers in Tennessee refused to accept fugitive slaves, most refrained from following the War Department recommendation that they determine the status of slaves under the Second Confiscation Act and issue freedom papers to the qualifying ones.[23] Left in a legal limbo between slavery and freedom, contrabands assumed the privileges of free men, much to the offense of prejudiced whites, like the editor who wrote: "We know of no persons who are so disgustingly presuming on their imaginary 'human and Divine rights and privileges' than the sable individuals." Simultaneously, Federals were depriving secessionists of their legal rights, sometimes in a manner calculated to make them feel lower than the contrabands. Soldiers sent the slaves of a leading Fayette County secessionist riding away in his fine carriage, an unprecedented dignity for the blacks. Proslavery whites deeply resented changes in slave status that seemed to come at their expense.[24]

The uncertain legal status of contrabands created problems for local government. Nashville and Memphis initially treated them as slaves. Police recorder courts fined or whipped runaways for such slave code violations as assembling, possessing weapons, hiring out their own time, and selling merchandise; the same courts fined whites and free blacks for harboring and selling liquor to fugitive slaves.[25] As the contraband population rapidly multiplied, a massive breakdown of old laws confronted civil authorities. Contrabands were forced to hire out their own time, sell merchandise, or steal to survive. Having rejected the bonds of slavery, they did not intend to respect other laws restricting their race. At the same time, whites found it difficult to coexist with these potential employees and customers without violating the slave code themselves. Proslavery traditions called for enforcement of the law; military rulers refused on the basis of expediency.

The first major clash between civil and military powers occurred in Memphis after Major General William T. Sherman, the post commander, assumed control over law enforcement in October 1862. On the grounds that all slaves in the city potentially could be free under the Second Confiscation Act, he ordered police to treat them as freedmen until federal courts ruled otherwise in individual cases. Sherman's de facto suspension of the slave code in Memphis did not arise from abolitionist impulses. Holding strong racial prejudices and believing that only courts could carry out confiscation, he had previously refused to consider all slaves freed by the act when his brother, a Republican politician, suggested he do so. The general shifted his position because of an intensely nationalistic contempt for secessionists, commitment to military obedience, and, most importantly, issuance of the Preliminary Emancipation Proclamation. He obeyed Lincoln's instructions for commanders to "observe, obey, and enforce" the Second Confiscation Act in a more extreme fashion than other generals.[26]

Judge John T. Swayne, of the Shelby County criminal court, quickly challenged Sherman's suspension of the slave code. In a grand jury charge, which opened with a ringing reaffirmation of proslavery ideology, Swayne demanded the continued indictment of code violators. Admitting that the federal government possessed the power to confiscate slaves, he denied that it

could destroy slave property through emancipation or the void-
ing of local laws. He privately hoped that test cases initiated in
his court would lead to a federal Supreme Court ruling on the
constitutionality of the Second Confiscation Act. In response,
Sherman took the position that "No Law of Tennessee [is] in
conflict with the Law of the United States for the latter is *the*
Law and if any Lawyer or Judge thinks different, the quicker he
gets out of the United States the Safer his Neck will be." The
general immediately notified Swayne that the army would not
permit convictions for violations of the suspended slave code;
the post's provost marshal added a threat of summary punishment for any attempt to try such cases. Effectively intimidated,
the judge admitted in his next grand jury charge that the court
must accept its current inability to prosecute laws he still considered to be valid.[27]

After Sherman left Memphis for a field command, the
municipal government continued to treat blacks as free except
in one important respect: the police recorder court revived
whipping sentences for convicted contrabands. In May 1863
the unionist city government prohibited public whippings
from drawing blood, which forced the recorder to replace
whippings with fines. One year later, the antislavery Memphis
Bulletin began a campaign for repeal of the municipal slave
code by falsely accusing the aldermen of secretly reenacting it.
In response, several city fathers attempted to repeal the code,
but a military government replaced them before the matter
reached a final vote.[28] Although the Memphis slave code stayed
on the books, it remained unenforced.

Nashville and the army clashed over the slave code shortly
after Rosecrans began admitting male contrabands through the
lines. Judge Manson M. Brien, of the Davidson County criminal court, wanted both to preserve the code and to avoid conflict with the military. He managed to circumvent trouble by
instructing the grand jury to present indictments only in cases

not involving the army's interests. Lacking Brien's tact, Police Recorder William Shane sentenced two contrabands to thirty-nine lashes each for holding a dance that was authorized by the post commander rather than city officials. Shane also fined a federal labor contractor for harboring fugitive slaves after the man rented rooms to contrabands he had hired. When the recorder arraigned a second government agent on the same charge, the army ordered him to stop prosecuting certain code violations.[29]

The author and terms of the order went unrecorded, but the court never again prosecuted the assembling, harboring, or employment of contrabands. It also stopped trying blacks for selling merchandise, provided they purchased licenses and did not include liquor in their wares. In June 1863 the disgruntled aldermen, guided by Judge Brien, asked the army either to place contrabands under military supervision or to permit full enforcement of the slave code, excepting the return of runaways to secessionist owners. The army refused to respond.[30]

Other developments in 1863 further undercut the slave code in Nashville. Andrew Johnson and several other unionists, urged on by Lincoln, publicly began to advocate abolition. Federals started enlisting and arming contrabands. The black community initiated a series of mass meetings to discuss race-related issues. These major violations of the code made any further enforcement awkward. After October 1863 Shane ceased issuing whipping sentences for contrabands. Brien capitulated in his next grand jury charge, which instructed panelists not to return indictments for any slave code violations: "It is not *practicable* or *expedient* to enforce it. To enforce this code as rebels would have us do, would cause great distress and inhumanity."[31] For practical purposes, the slave code had become inoperable in Nashville by the end of 1863.

Except for the situation in the state's two largest cities, little is known about local law enforcement during the war. Most courts in rural areas suspended operations until peace returned. A major incident occurred in Columbia during 1864, when a magistrate sentenced William Jordan, a contraband, to twenty-five lashes for educating slaves in violation of a town ordinance. Because the post commander had granted Jordan permission to hold the school, military authorities arrested the magistrate and two other town officials on charges of assault and battery. A military court convicted the three, but General Rousseau disapproved the proceedings on a technicality (the court failed to determine whether the defendants pleaded guilty or not) and released them.[32]

On September 7, shortly after the Columbia case, Military Governor Johnson acted to eliminate the problems caused by the slave code. Having campaigned for a year to turn unionists against slavery, he apparently believed sufficient progress had been made to suspend the code, which he did by ordering the courts to treat slaves as free blacks. A test of the proclamation's legality came immediately in the case of *McClay v. Driver*. Henry Driver's slave had run away and obtained a job at Robert McClay's sawmill. Driver obtained a court order from a Davidson County magistrate for the slave's wages, but McClay cited Johnson's proclamation in appealing the ruling before a circuit court. Manson M. Brien, whom Johnson had recently appointed to preside over the court, charged the jury to uphold the proclamation. When they decided in Driver's favor instead, Brien, holding that the jury had ignored his instructions, overruled the verdict.[33]

Suspension of the slave code still left the contrabands liable to similar laws governing free blacks. However, the army overrode municipal ordinances against black education by granting protection to the schools. By 1864 unionist governments in Nashville and Memphis ignored the state ban on black merchandising.[34] When Wade Hickman, a contraband leader in

Nashville, applied for a liquor license that year, Johnson ended the city's prosecution of black liquor dealers by issuing permits on his own authority. In a few military trials, the army accepted black testimony against whites. The sole legal restriction enforced without abridgment during the war was the ban on miscegenation.[35]

Because of Confederate defeats in Tennessee, white civilians lost both the rule of law and control of their government. Open conflict between contrabands and whites resulted in both sides turning to the federal conquerors for help. Inasmuch as contrabands supported the invaders and most whites did not, the army gradually suspended the legal barriers constricting the status of slaves. Without maintenance by the ruling power and without control over slaves' minds, the institution's future grew dim. One frustrated slaveholder accurately described the situation: "To say that I may take my negroes home if they wish to go or may control them if they [are] willing I should, is to say that slavery ceases to exist except at the will of the slave."[36]

4

Black Ghettos and Contraband Camps

Slaves ran away in quest of freedom, but that promising beacon all too often led to the torments of poverty. Possessing little property, they forsook even a regular subsistence in leaving their owners. Unless they stole from their masters, they lacked significant resources beyond their ability to work.[1] Some compromised by entering new dependency relationships, but most tried to live as independently as possible.

One type of contraband, slaves abandoned by masters, enjoyed an opportunity to achieve a comfortable self-sufficiency by assuming control over their owners' homesteads and property. A slave named William, left behind when his master fled south, operated a Lauderdale County farm for his own profit and even hired two white field hands for a time. However, abandoned slaves who lived in combat zones found farming virtually impossible. They suffered from the loss of essential animals and provisions to both armies, not to mention the constant risk of personal harm. Many eventually were forced to flee plantations for towns.[2]

Federally garrisoned towns offered contrabands their best chance for safety and jobs. At first, all but impressed laborers needed to find living accommodations on their own. Federals later created refugee camps, but, according to every estimate made of the two largest contraband populations, those in

46

Memphis and Nashville, two-thirds or more continued to live on their own.[3] The numbers of urban blacks rose dramatically as footloose slaves moved into outbuildings, abandoned homes, and rented rooms.[4] When the supply of existing structures was exhausted, shantytowns sprang up on empty lots and the edges of towns. These wooden shacks ranged from the comfortable and stoutly built to the flimsy and windowless. Because of a local shortage of wood in 1865, many Chattanooga contrabands were required to live in dirty sod huts. Water and sanitation arrangements were extremely poor: Memphis blacks drank impure bayou water, and those in Nashville improvised aboveground privies on a vacant lot. Overcrowded housing, which accommodated as many as six families in one room, further endangered health.[5]

Urban free blacks had never before concentrated in neighborhoods of their own. Therefore, the shantytowns became Tennessee's first black ghettos. The contrabands' virtual freedom eliminated most distinctions between the two castes. Although a few free blacks tried to maintain differences, the two groups usually mingled as one and shared an ethnic community's special sense of camaraderie. In these neighborhoods, fugitive slaves encountered new ideas, people, and activities; they could openly operate their own schools, churches, and businesses. Unfortunately, urban life also bred vice in gambling dens, saloons, and brothels; the problems of drunkenness, brawling, and adultery frequently showed up in police recorder court.[6] Thus the ghettos offered new opportunities for either personal growth or decadence.

As urban contrabands multiplied, new arrivals faced an increasingly difficult time obtaining steady employment, and the war inflated the prices of necessities. Some turned to begging or crime; a few actually stole vegetables at gunpoint. Others starved rather than steal, like the family a Northern philanthropist discovered one winter's day lying on their floor in a

47

stupor. The previous day, they had burned their bedstead and eaten their last food.[7] Ghetto dwellers quickly learned that poverty stood ready to destroy their dream of independence.

As an alternative means of survival, a minority of Tennessee contrabands became dependent upon the army. Many runaways fled directly to the Federals, but, as a chaplain observed, "often they met prejudice against their color more bitter than that they left behind." Furthermore, a campaigning army could not always provide protection and food for a long train of contrabands.[8]

As the first commander to stop excluding fugitive slaves, General Grant was the first to confront the problem of providing for them. For a time, he shipped them to the Midwest, but the War Department's sensitivity to Northern racial prejudices halted that practice. Grant then established a contraband camp at Grand Junction, Tennessee. Mixing humanitarianism and pragmatism, he offered food, shelter, and medical care in return for labor, initially in the harvesting of abandoned cotton fields for the federal government. The War Department readily approved the program because other commanders had opened similar camps along the southeastern coastline.[9] Wherever the government started the camps, it undertook a significant responsibility for the welfare of its contraband allies.

The superintendent of Grant's first camp was a young Presbyterian minister, Chaplain John Eaton, of the 27th Ohio Infantry. He had not been an abolitionist before the war, but the more he saw of slavery, the more it disgusted him. Considering himself far more practical than most reformers, he supported emancipation for reasons both of humanitarianism and military expediency.[10]

Eaton's assignment made him unpopular with many whites at Grand Junction. Most soldiers resented being detailed to him. John N. Waddell, the local Presbyterian minister, took offense at the chaplain's naive request for aid: "I don't conceive that any Southern man is under the least moral obligation to help the negro-stealers plan how they shall take care of them." Confederate guerrillas tried to assassinate Eaton and did kill one of his assistants. Eaton's dedicated persistence impressed Grant, who expanded the chaplain's responsibilities to include all contrabands behind the general's lines. The operation later acquired the name Freedmen's Department of the Department of the Tennessee.[11]

The Grand Junction camp came to an abrupt end in January 1863, when Confederates flanked Grant's advance units in Mississippi and endangered the rear in West Tennessee. In the rush to move contrabands to safety in Memphis, Eaton observed much disorder: "Their terror of being left behind made them swarm over the passenger and freight cars, clinging to every available space and even crouching on the roofs." Tribulations continued after they reached Memphis, for the new camp was still under construction. Eaton's charges suffered from unusually severe winter weather, for they were crowded into an inadequate number of tents. They called their new home Camp Holly Springs because of a large influx of contrabands from that Mississippi town. In early 1863 Eaton expanded the facilities at Memphis by opening another camp at President's Island and by assuming supervision over a contraband village known as Shiloh.[12]

For a short time in 1863, a network of contraband camps extended across West Tennessee (see table 4). New camps appeared at Grand Junction, La Grange, Bolivar, Jackson, Fort Pillow, and Island No. 10.[13] Later in the year, the army removed its garrisons from the first four places and shipped the contrabands to Memphis. In April 1864 a Confederate attack destroyed the Fort Pillow camp and scattered the survivors. Two months later, Eaton moved the Island No. 10 contrabands to Helena, Arkansas, to fill jobs there.[14] As the West Tennessee system shrank down to the Memphis camps, Freedmen's Department officials decided to concentrate all their charges at President's Island because of its isolated location a mile and a half below the city. The island would not only provide more safety in the event of a Confederate attack on Memphis but would also separate contrabands from what officials viewed as immoral influences in the city and army camps. Numerous difficulties delayed completion of the relocation until November 1864. Several spring floods prevented the enlarged camp from becoming a success.[15]

The long retention of policies excluding contrabands from the lines in Middle Tennessee delayed the official inauguration of a camp system there. Even after Military Governor Johnson endorsed emancipation, he wanted slaves to stay with masters, preferably on a wage basis. As a Democrat and a self-made man, he firmly believed in governmental laissez-faire and personal self-reliance. Johnson opposed the appropriation of plantations for contraband camps for fear of heightening racial tensions. He suspected that camp paternalism would attract "only the dross" and preserve their "squalid debased condition." On the grounds that charity would only encourage resourceless slaves to run away, he refused to issue tents to shelterless contrabands during the winter of late 1863.[16]

Out of pity for the suffering contrabands, post commanders established unauthorized camps at Fort Donelson, Gallatin, Murfreesboro, Dechard, and Pulaski.[17] Officials recruiting blacks in Nashville housed and fed some enlistees' families in an abandoned chapel. Johnson himself permitted a few blacks to room and board with white war refugees in the state capitol building. Most contrabands in Middle Tennessee, however, were forced to survive on their own resources during 1862–63.[18]

On January 26, 1864, a post commander shipped all contrabands at Stevenson, Alabama, to Nashville without notifying federal authorities there. Reuben D. Mussey, a recruiter of black troops, found them standing outside the railroad station in the cold. He immediately complained to General Grant, who, as head of the new Military Division of the Mississippi, now commanded most federal forces in the West. Grant ordered Nashville's post commander to provide for the contrabands. Shortly afterward, while visiting the area, Adjutant General Thomas established a large contraband camp outside the city to serve as a central depot for all unemployed blacks in the Department of the Cumberland.[19]

The adjutant general appointed as camp superintendent Captain Ralph Hunt, a Kentuckian who was supervising the Stevenson contrabands. Hunt soon abandoned the central depot concept and opened a branch camp at Clarksville upon request of the post's commander. Within a few months, Hunt assumed control over the existing camps at Gallatin and Pulaski. Because Middle Tennessee, unlike West Tennessee, maintained a wide network of garrisons throughout its occupation, it operated a large system of camps that gave blacks more inducement to escape slavery.[20]

Hunt showed little sympathy for contrabands, and, shortly after his enlistment ended in June 1864, investigators discovered that he had embezzled some camp supplies. The next superintendent was Colonel Robert W. Barnard, of the 101st Colored Infantry, an honest if unimaginative man who was firmly committed to emancipation. Calling himself Superintendent of Freedmen for the Department of the Cumberland, he increased his responsibilities by taking control of the contraband camp at Fort Donelson and by opening a new one at Hendersonville. Although most directors of Freedmen's Departments publicized their work, this former businessman devoted himself solely to the everyday operations of his camps.[21]

Barnard faced but did not surmount a major crisis when Major General John B. Hood led a Confederate invasion of Middle Tennessee in late 1864. Contrabands in the Pulaski

51

camp and many slaves in Hood's path fled to the state capital and swamped the Nashville camp until it was safe to leave in early January. Misery pervaded life at the overcrowded site. At first, the weather was bitterly cold, and the area lacked firewood; when the temperature later rose, the camp sank into six inches of mud, which was particularly bad for those housed in tents. One man went around begging for scarce wood planks so his children would not need to sleep in the mud. Approximately one-sixth of the contrabands died in the three weeks after Hood's defeat. Because of this debacle, Adjutant General Thomas designated Colonel Mussey as supervisor of contrabands in East and Middle Tennessee for the last months of the war.[22]

No contraband camp system appeared in East Tennessee, where, after all, the slave population was small. The director of black recruiting in Knoxville began to construct a camp but abandoned the effort when General Sherman prohibited issues of rations to East Tennessee civilians during his 1864 campaign against Atlanta. During Hood's later invasion, federal authorities in Chattanooga established a refugee camp for both races. When the Confederates retreated, the post commander shipped unemployed contrabands to the Nashville camp and utilized the rest to build a black settlement across the Tennessee River from Chattanooga.[23]

In Middle and West Tennessee, the two Freedmen's Departments faced a difficult task in providing for contrabands. Camp superintendents could never plan ahead because camp populations fluctuated unpredictably. Enlistment, employment, dissatisfaction, and death constantly reduced the numbers, but, as table 4 illustrates, gains usually exceeded losses.[24] Desperate need brought contrabands into camps, but their very entry made it harder for superintendents to meet that need.

The only detailed description left by a contraband of life in a Tennessee camp is grim. Nat Black lived in the Nashville camp

Table 4. Contraband Camp Populations, 1863–1865

	March '63	Fall '63	Winter '64	Spring '64	Summer '64	Fall '64	January '65	March '65	April '65	June '65
WEST TENNESSEE										
Grand Junction	1,708									
La Grange	750									
Bolivar	1,131									
Jackson	800									
Fort Pillow		311								
Island No. 10		839	968							
Camp Shiloh	1,236	600*				} 1,932				
Camp Holly Springs		751	3,106	1,854						
President's Island		1,540	1,038	799	3,000*		2,900*		1,568	
MIDDLE TENNESSEE										
Nashville			560	677		479	1,000*			481
Clarksville					1,078	1,122	1,300*	2,000*		1,365
Fort Donelson			300*						1,500*	391
Pulaski			920	1,712		1,500*		275	325	
Gallatin					273	264	462		337	356
Murfreesboro			2,000*							
Hendersonville							700*			448

*Estimated figures

during most of its existence. In contrast to the rural isolation in which he had grown up, he noted that the camp contained "worlds o' colored people." He slept in a dirt-floored tent with three blankets; the clothing allotment was not always enough to keep him warm. Cooks issued rations twice a day to family heads, but the beef was "so old . . . that when thrown against a wall it would splatter like mud." Many died from disease; lice tormented the survivors. Black retained no happy memories of the place.[25]

In caring for contrabands, the two Freedmen's Departments relied on cooperation from military authorities and on the be-

Table 5. Freedmen's Aid Societies
in Tennessee, 1863–1865

Name	Places of Activity									
	Chattanooga	Clarksville	Gallatin	Hendersonville	Island No. 10	Knoxville	Memphis	Murfreesboro	Nashville	Pulaski
Religious Societies										
American Baptist Home Mission Society							X		X	
American Missionary Association (interdenominational)	X						X		X	
Association of Friends for the Aid and Elevation of the Freedmen									X	
Indiana Yearly Meeting of Friends Executive Committee for the Relief of Colored Freedmen									X	X
United Presbyterian Church's Missionary Board					X			X		X

54

Table 5, continued

Name	Chattanooga	Clarksville	Gallatin	Hendersonville	Island No. 10	Knoxville	Memphis	Murfreesboro	Nashville	Pulaski
Secular Societies										
Contraband Relief Commission (Cincinnati)					X					
Indiana Freedmen's Aid Commission (Indianapolis)	X							X	X	
Northwestern Freedmen's Aid Commission (Chicago)				X			X		X	X
Pennsylvania Freedmen's Relief Association (Philadelphia)								X	X	
Western Freedmen's Aid Commission (Cincinnati)		X	X		X		X	X	X	
Black Societies										
Black Odd Fellows							X			
Good Samaritan Society									X	
Order of Sons of Relief									X	
Sons of Ham							X			

nevolence of freedmen's aid societies. During the war, a number of new philanthropic organizations appeared in the North and a few among Southern blacks. Table 5 lists those that were active in Tennessee.[26]

Societies helped primarily by donating clothing to replace the tattered garments worn by fugitive slaves. Military officials lacked authority to purchase clothing for contrabands and could only issue uniforms rejected by quartermasters or taken from deceased Federals.[27] Because only men wore the uniforms, the needs of women and children were the greatest, especially in winter. Freedmen's aid societies sent large quantities of garments into Tennessee, but could not always keep up with demand. After spending a long winter's day handing out clothing to children, one agent recorded that "a crowd of crying disappointed ones had to go unsupplied."[28]

Eaton and Barnard sought to make the contraband camps as self-sufficient as possible, an aim shared by the residents. Late in the war, both directors obtained equipment that contrabands could use to produce their own clothing. Black women in three new industrial schools at Memphis made garments from cloth sent by freedmen's aid societies, and the Pulaski camp acquired looms to weave its own cloth. The Clarksville camp produced both clothes and shoes.[29]

A serious housing shortage resulted from the concentration of contrabands in urban centers. Except for abandoned buildings, only camps offered free housing. Superintendents lacked the means to predict future housing needs. The La Grange camp became so overcrowded that newcomers received only a blanket and advice to build themselves a bush-arbor shelter. In the summer of 1864 War Department investigators blamed the Nashville camp superintendent for failing to provide sufficient housing; the records show that he actually had constructed new buildings as fast as possible during the spring, but could never keep up with increasing demand.[30] Severe housing problems also resulted from military events, as when Confederate raiders burned the Pulaski camp in 1864. The worst shortages occurred when Confederate invasions forced the midwinter evacuation of contrabands from rural areas into Memphis in January 1863, and into Nashville in December 1864.[31]

Camp housing typically began with vacant buildings and tents. Tents eventually became too worn to provide shelter and were replaced by log or plank buildings, usually erected by the contrabands themselves.[32] Visitors gave low ratings to the log cabins at President's Island and Island No. 10 because of poor ventilation, insufficient lighting, and cramped quarters; buildings at Pulaski and Clarksville gained praise for solid construction and comfortableness.[33] Differences in housing quality probably arose from variations in contrabands' building skills, superintendents' abilities to supervise construction, and available supplies.

Like housing materials, much of the food came from military stores. When Eaton opened his first camp, he had to negotiate with Grant's commissary about the content and amount of rations. Eaton believed that the result, a slightly reduced version of the generous ration issued to soldiers, approximated the quantity of food slaves received.[34] In January 1864 Secretary of War Stanton set a uniform contraband ration, containing significantly less food than Eaton's ration (except for military laborers, who received the same ration as soldiers). Lorenzo Thomas pleaded with Stanton, but could not budge him from the retrenchment measure.[35]

Contraband camps could not always rely upon military commissaries for food. Red tape occasionally choked the flow of rations, and armies in the field always enjoyed first access to supplies. During his Atlanta campaign, General Sherman cut off rations for civilian refugees east and south of Nashville.[36] Camps fortunately could avail themselves of several alternate food sources: abandoned plantation storerooms; nearby wildlife; and their own gardens, for which freedmen's aid societies furnished seeds and equipment. Consequently, the residents usually did not suffer from food shortages.[37]

Serious health problems resulted from overcrowding and poor facilities in shantytowns and contraband camps. Contemporaries estimated that the death toll during the winter of 1862–63 alone ran as high as 1,200 in Memphis and 1,400 in Nashville.[38] Freedmen's aid societies sent some medical supplies south, but not to the extent of their clothing contributions. Contraband women volunteered as nurses in camp hospitals, which existed at Grand Junction, La Grange, Bolivar, Memphis, Island No. 10, Nashville, and Murfreesboro. Other camps, except that at Gallatin, which lacked any professional medical care, probably drew upon the services of army doctors in local garrisons.[39]

During the summer of 1864, Congress eliminated funds for the medical care of contrabands from the military budget. Eaton's medical director used a freedmen's fund, raised by taxing employed contrabands' wages, to continue the hospital at Memphis. Records do not reveal what other hospitals did. Aroused by the problem, Adjutant General Thomas immediately began negotiating with the surgeon general and Treasury Secretary William P. Fessenden to find alternative funding. The surgeon general agreed to supply the hospitals with medicines from government laboratories at cost, and Fessenden consented to cover the expenses as part of his administration of abandoned Southern farms (the lessees usually hired contraband laborers). Stanton, however, disliked the scheme and revoked it. The hospitals did not receive federal funding again until the fall of 1865.[40]

Contraband hospitals encountered more problems than finances. Wards were often unsanitary and uncomfortable. An inspector described the dirt-floored buildings of the Memphis Freedmen's Hospital as "scarcely fit to be occupied by animals." Large tents in which the hospital placed surplus patients became so worn at one time that the patients suffered from exposure to the weather. Hospitals also lacked sufficient staffs, and untrained contraband nurses sometimes administered the wrong medicines. Despite serious shortcomings, hospitals made some contribution to reducing the high mortality rates of urban contrabands.[41]

Freedom cost contrabands much in terms of material comfort. Two Northern philanthropists commented that "it does seem a pity they should have to live in such a miserable style, when they were anticipating so much." Yet, like George Knox, most contrabands concluded: "If we have made our bed hard, we would lay on it, and never go back until we were taken or times were better."[42] Most survived amidst destitution through their own efforts and luck; the rest sustained themselves with help from the Freedmen's Departments and freedmen's aid societies. Even when living in contraband camps, they worked toward self-sufficiency. Masters could not understand the abandonment of a guaranteed subsistence for an abstract good, freedom; yet, contrabands believed that one key to a better future was personal independence.

5

Beginning of Economic and Social Reconstruction

As slavery began to unravel amidst civil war, contrabands and free blacks pressed for new privileges. To the pragmatists among them, gains seemed possible. For the visionaries, like a preacher in Nashville, it was a matter of providential justice: "De Lord He was wid us, and wouldn't let us be 'pressed no more. . . . [We shall] not be robbed ob de rights de Lord hab gib us—and the year of jubilee *is* come."[1] Blacks sought to exercise all the privileges enjoyed by whites: the prerogatives of wage laborers, entrepreneurial opportunity, religious independence, familial security, education, the right to bear arms, and the franchise. In trying to cause whites to reevaluate their race's status, contrabands asserted a sense of human dignity against racism.

As a weak minority, blacks needed toleration and sometimes active support from the ruling federal authorities. However, the Lincoln administration gave the army little direction for wartime reconstruction of race relations. Most commanders ignored contrabands except in matters involving military expediency, which after all was the army's first concern.[2] Within the Freedmen's Departments and the freedmen's aid societies, sympathetic whites worked for most of the changes blacks wanted, but not always to the same extent or as quickly.

White antislavery reformers fell into two ideological groups.

In Tennessee one of them included George L. Stearns and Reuben D. Mussey, directors of black recruiting in Middle Tennessee, as well as Asa S. Fiske, a Freedmen's Department official in West Tennessee. Except for a deep commitment to racial equality, they maintained a Jeffersonian laissez-faire philosophy. Holding that the accomplishment of equality required only liberation, education, and gainful employment, they granted that freedmen would need some guidance and charitable support but wanted all help and regulation minimized to make sure the blacks would stand on their own. "No man is a swimmer until Cork Jackets are off him—as well as manacles," Mussey wrote. "Do let him exercise his selfhood and Manhood, working out his own destiny." These reformers expected individual contrabands to prove themselves or suffer the consequences of failure.[3]

Adjutant General Lorenzo Thomas and General Superintendent John Eaton of the Freedmen's Department for the Department of the Tennessee subscribed to a different philosophy. Although they did not want freedmen to become permanently dependent on patrons, they called for major transitional programs of care, control, and guidance. This group of reformers advocated paternalism in the belief that slavery had caused degradation into the depths of irresponsibility, ignorance, and immorality. "It is not like a husbandman who takes a field in the Spring to cultivate, before the weeds start," the superintendent of the Fort Donelson contraband camp contended, "but like taking the field with the corn choked with weeds until it is almost ruined." Eaton considered it "inadmissable to throw them, many of them as it were, in a state of childhood, upon their own undirected resources." White reformers could elevate them because, in his opinion, slaves habitually depended upon whites.[4] Although paternalists would deny it, a prejudicial condescension ran through their programs. Laissez-faire critics pointed out that proslavery theorists had likewise held that blacks needed and benefited from paternalistic treatment. Although lacking the laissez-faire reformers' respect for the abilities of blacks, the paternalistic group practiced generosity to the needy, unlike their counterparts.

Paternalistic policies dominated reconstruction programs during the war, probably because of the concern about social and economic order behind federal lines. Moreover, insofar as the Mississippi Valley was concerned, the most powerful official involved with contraband affairs was Adjutant General Thomas. In Middle Tennessee, Stearns, Mussey, and the unphilosophical Robert W. Barnard only moderated the policy. After all, both groups shared the same goal of gaining a meaningful freedom for the slaves. In actual practice, they differed primarily over how much should be done for the contrabands and for how long. Open clashes over reform philosophy occurred elsewhere but not in Tennessee.[5]

While paternalistic ideology helped to circumscribe federal reconstruction during the war, the blacks' lack of power hindered their own efforts to gain equality. A common mistaken notion is that contrabands so lacked confidence in each other that they depended upon white guidance.[6] Admittedly, whites controlled some crucial resources upon which practical blacks would need to rely, but the commitment of the contrabands to independence dominates the evidence from Tennessee. Because blacks wanted aid from whites yet often remained suspicious of them, it is scarcely surprising that they tried to manipulate reformers, just as they had their masters. Not always in full unison, but together, contrabands and reformers would lay foundations for new black roles.

Wartime Economic Reconstruction

From the beginning of federal occupation, disloyal slaves attempted to reconstruct the Southern labor system. Some coerced their owners into compensatory arrangements, while others ran away seeking new opportunities. The flight of many domestic slaves and the boom conditions after federal occupation created a number of jobs in the towns. Contrabands, sensitive about their self-declared status as free laborers, readily shifted jobs when an employer seemed to infringe upon their dignity. One black arraigned his employer in the Nashville police recorder court for throwing a bucket of water on him. Some valued their independence so highly that they chose to survive through high-paying odd jobs, especially in moving goods, rather than through regular employment.[7]

Job opportunities did not ensure entry into the free labor system. Not all contrabands could find work, and many were impressed into military labor gangs without compensation. During the first years of federal occupation, the employed ones could not always collect their pay. Because slaves enjoyed no legal right to wages or to testify against whites in court, employers could safely withhold compensation.[8] Completion of a metamorphosis that had begun in the labor system during 1862–63 was uncertain.

The federal army had the power to help, and the Freedmen's Department in West Tennessee pioneered several economic reconstruction programs. Eaton, like most reformers, fundamentally believed in the Work Ethic, which emphasized the values of hard work, self-reliance, sobriety, and thrift; he also accepted a corollary obligation to improve one's economic condition. In his opinion, slavery had prevented slaves from internalizing these values: "Beyond receiving punishment when their task was unperformed or leisure if accomplished before its time, they saw little relation between their industry and their comfort; not their labor but their masters clothed and fed them."[9]

Assuming that the only incentive of slaves to work had been the lash, most camp superintendents feared that contrabands would equate liberty with idleness and concluded that they needed moral instruction. Laissez-faire reformer Asa S. Fiske, on the other hand, held that they wanted to earn a living and only needed a chance to do so. All the superintendents expected their charges to live up to the Work Ethic, lest, as Eaton put it, contrabands "bring a disgrace upon the President & his policy." Eaton also knew that self-sufficient camps would save the government money and weaken the Confederacy by encouraging more slaves to run away.[10] Expediency and idealism combined with theories about slavery to make work programs imperative.

Blacks who could not find employment usually entered contraband camps. Seeing them as wards, Eaton sought to end their dependence upon the army and to transform them into model free laborers. He used a preferential distribution of donated clothing to reward those who demonstrated self-reliance, hard work, and sobriety.[11] Despite superintendents' apprehensions, contrabands showed no reluctance to work hard. In most camps, they built their own buildings, raised their food, and cultivated cash crops.[12] Various camps also ran firewood services, blacksmith shops, gristmills, clothing manufactories, sawmills, a brick kiln, and a shoe shop. Still, most camps lacked enough work to keep all the residents busy.[13]

Contrabands usually could not earn money from work done inside the camp. Woodchoppers received small incentive payments, and in 1865 the President's Island and Pulaski superintendents experimented with wage systems. Most superintendents expected service in return for subsistence. Doubting the thriftiness of their charges, they placed camp profits in freedmen's funds, which they spent as they saw fit for the group's benefit.[14] Thus, camp work programs stressed communal rather than individual self-reliance. Most residents must have considered a temporary supervised dependency either satisfactory or tolerable, but some yearned for more independence. For example, the Fort Donelson contrabands sowed gardens in family plots instead of the usual communal one when illness incapacitated their superintendent during a spring planting.[15]

While camps provided work for relatively few blacks, the federal army needed many laborers. Officers hired some as servants, often offering only food and clothing as pay. Federals forcibly impressed many from contraband camps and ghettos during the early war years. In the constant search for more laborers, patrols raided barber shops, churches, and even a Fourth of July celebration.[16]

Federal soldiers gloated that "we drill one hour in the evening and lay in the shade the rest of the day while the negroes are doing the work." Although the army did not whip the unpaid laborers, it often exploited and abused them as if they were slaves. According to Major Stearns, the lot of impressed blacks was particularly bad in Nashville, where they often had to sleep without blankets, fire, or shelter. The army fed them bread its commissary had rejected. Primarily because of poor provisioning, more than a fourth of the blacks impressed in Nashville during 1862 and 1863 died, and public awareness of this made it hard for the Federals to find replacements.[17]

During the summer of 1862 Congress permitted the army to hire the slaves of secessionists for a $10 monthly wage, but contraband laborers in Tennessee received no pay that year—though careful work records were kept—because officers refused to assume the authority to judge masters' political allegiance.[18] Change came first in West Tennessee, where Eaton persuaded Grant sometime in 1863 to pay black workers regardless of their owners' politics. In Middle Tennessee, a severe need for laborers in January 1863 prompted General Rosecrans to order pay for the black hands, except those belonging to proven unionists. However, many hiring officers refused to pay without explicit guidelines from the War Department. The Engineering Department, which used the largest number of blacks, was notorious for relying upon impressed and unpaid labor.[19]

The mistreatment of impressed blacks in Nashville appalled Stearns. To prove that wage labor could successfully replace impressment, he found 228 contrabands who volunteered to work during October 1863 for a $10 wage, rations, and exemption from future impressment. After their supervisor reported that they worked twice as hard as impressed laborers, Stearns succeeded in convincing Military Governor Johnson to pay men then being impressed to build the Northwestern Railroad. The major's efforts failed to obtain wages for other impressed personnel and could not stop impressments. General George H. Thomas actually prevented several of Stearns's volunteers from receiving wages by having their owners paid instead. In December a quartermaster's impressment carried off some of the volunteers in violation of their exemptions.[20]

By taking some slaves who had stayed with their masters, the Quartermaster Department aroused proslavery General Lovell H. Rousseau to prohibit impressments on the grounds of respect for the owners' needs. No more impressments occurred in Nashville until the emergency created by Hood's invasion. After Rousseau's order, the Engineer and Quartermaster departments could only keep black laborers by paying them.[21] The army compensated few men for work performed under impressment and never paid them as much as white employees. Although a number of contrabands throughout the state held remunerative government jobs by 1864, most positions could not outlast postwar demobilization.[22] To achieve a long-term solution for the economic problems of contrabands, federal officials would need to initiate programs dealing with the private employment of blacks.

Early in 1863, thinking particularly about those who lived by odd jobs or crime, Eaton drew up a supervised employment plan for contrabands living outside camps. To meet the twin goals of social control and economic reconstruction, he proposed a pass system. Employed blacks would need to register with the Freedmen's Department, which would supervise the fulfillment of labor contracts. Just as antebellum patrols had arrested slaves traveling without passes, federal patrols would seize blacks without employment papers and detain them in contraband camps. Concerned about vagrancy, the Memphis post commander instituted the pass system in July 1863, but did not give the Freedmen's Department supervisory power over contraband contracts.[23]

Blacks suspected that a reenslavement plot lay behind the order because it required them to have a white employer. After trying in vain to register as independent day laborers, they circumvented the rules by hiring whites to pose as their employers. By October the post provost marshal tired of the farce and revoked all registrations. To allay fears of reenslavement, he allowed new registrations under either white or black employers. In an attempt to eliminate fakery, he announced that employers would henceforth be responsible for the good conduct of contraband employees. Contrabands who lived by irregular work or crime continued to enter false registrations; when sent to President's Island, they found ways of escaping. Similar efforts in Nashville to intern all but regularly employed blacks fared no better.[24]

Brigadier General Eleazer A. Paine, Gallatin post commander, established the first supervised contract program for Tennessee contrabands in the spring of 1863. When runaway slaves swamped his headquarters, he urged them to make compensatory agreements with their owners and denied rations to those who refused a job. Paine promised masters that, if they paid wages, he would force slaves to stay at work. His printed contracts required owners to provide employees with everything a slave received (food, clothes, shelter, and medical care) plus a wage, originally fixed at a low $8 a month for men and $5 for women but later left up to the contracting parties. In January 1864 Rousseau reported what he called Paine's "flagrant usurpation" to General George H. Thomas and won revocation of the contracts. Shortly afterward, Adjutant General Lorenzo Thomas ordered them reinstated.[25]

By early 1864 contract labor systems existed in most federal occupation zones. Under Stanton's orders, the adjutant general had organized an experimental program during 1863 in the area around Vicksburg, Mississippi. Because Thomas believed that the resolution of the slavery issue ultimately depended on how contrabands adjusted to the free labor system, he sought to ensure success through coercive supervision. He had as many camp members as possible contracted at expediently low rates ($7 a month for men and $5 for women, plus room and board in both cases) to Mississippi unionists and to Northern lessees of abandoned plantations. The adjutant general wanted all contrabands whom the army could not use to be employed privately. Then the contraband camp would function only as a temporary refuge for new runaways and as a poorhouse for the unemployable.[26]

Thomas extended this program to Eaton's department in November 1863 and to Hunt's contraband camp at Nashville in February 1864. After restoring Paine's contracts and beating off a Treasury Department attempt to take over the program, he issued a new set of rules on March 11, 1864, for contraband contracts in the Military Division of the Mississippi. Bowing to the Treasury's pressure for higher wages, he raised the minimum monthly rates to $10 for men and $7 for women, both of whom received food, housing, clothing, and medical care. Employees earned no pay when sick and could be fined for "indolence, insolence, disobedience of orders, and crime." Distrusting their ability to be self-reliant, thrifty, and hardworking, Thomas encouraged employers to withhold at least half their pay until year's end.[27] For most of the year, contract laborers would be almost as dependent as slaves or contraband camp residents.

The adjutant general also instituted repressive behavioral rules copied from regulations issued by the federal commander in Louisiana to keep that state's near-majority of blacks under control. Contract laborers could not leave employers' premises, sell merchandise, purchase liquor, or possess guns without permission from an officer who was called the "Provost Marshal of Freedmen." The provisions were distinctly reminiscent of the slave code, the major difference being that the army alone possessed the power to inflict physical punishment. Thomas used the Louisiana rules' justification: "Labor is a public duty and idleness and vagrancy a crime." Believing that both contrabands and employers needed supervision during the transition to a free labor system, he created the provost marshals of freedmen to enforce fulfillment of contract obligations.[28]

During the spring of 1864 the contract labor program boomed in Tennessee. Eaton had originally planned a gradual introduction of wages for contrabands but accepted the adjutant general's more direct program and then added a 10 percent tax on monthly pay over $6. Receipts went into the freedmen's fund in the belief that this would teach contrabands their obligations to society.[29] The Reverend Abner D. Olds, Camp Holly Springs superintendent, responded enthusiastically to the contract labor system, which he called "a blessing." He hoped it would end the demoralizing idleness and poverty of camp life. Federal authorities, concerned about vagrancy, rounded up the unemployed contrabands of Memphis and Nashville in an effort to force them into contract labor.[30] While paternalistic officials in West Tennessee fixed wages at the minimum amounts recommended by the adjutant general, the influence of Mussey's laissez-faire philosophy probably explains why Middle Tennessee wages rose freely above that level.[31]

One historian has argued that the establishment of contract labor systems marked a crucial turning point in reconstruction because they locked blacks into economic dependence, whereas continued stress on contraband camp systems might have led to independent communities of black landholders. Furthermore, Eaton has been accused of abandoning paternalistic reform for military expediency when he endorsed the contract labor system.[32] This interpretation needs qualification. The choice made by most Tennessee contrabands not to enter camps also played a major role in undermining chances that the camps could have become federal reservations for blacks. Eaton's acceptance of the contract labor system represented only a shift in policy emphasis, for, though benevolence declined, control and guidance—the other key elements of paternalism—remained.

The adjutant general's contract labor system presumed that most blacks would not improve their economic condition quickly. By efforts to inculcate contrabands with the Work Ethic and to secure their wages, federal officials sought to encourage the most energetic to rise financially. In some occupied areas, the army leased abandoned farms to selected contrabands, but no evidence of that has been found for Tennessee. In general, the emphasis remained upon a minimum income, which under Thomas's new rules approximated the average $11.94 plus board received monthly by male, white farm hands in Tennessee during 1860.[33] While economic mobility would be difficult on those terms, the prejudice and distrust permeating the contract labor system also guaranteed the continued exploitation and subordination of blacks.

Inevitably some employers defrauded contract laborers of pay, but victims did not take this complacently. The provost marshal of freedmen in West Tennessee had to deal with so many complaints that he needed a special commissioner to assist him; Gallatin and Pulaski post commanders were forced to appoint similar officials to supervise contract settlements in the fall of 1864.[34]

As blacks had been wary of Eaton's pass system in 1863, so contrabands suspected the contract labor program might restore slavery. One woman observed that, after her former owner hired her family, he worked them as hard as before and still required them to address his family members as "master" and "mistress." Contrabands deeply resented the assumption, commonly held by both proslavery Tennesseans and paternalistic reformers, that blacks would not work unless forced to do so. Moses Battle, of Nashville, chided a Northern philanthropist: "Dunno what fer, sah, anybody tink dat. De culled folks, what been a keepin up de country. Wen da had to work all day for de masters, da work o' nights and Sundays to make a lettle something for da selves. Now wen its all day to da selves dunno what fer da lie down and starve."[35]

Some contrabands entertained hopes and ambitions that none of the federal work programs fulfilled, for they wanted economic improvement without ever being subordinated to whites again. Abandoned rural slaves ran their owners' farms for their own profit, and enterprising urban contrabands founded a variety of small businesses. Craftsmen produced chairs, barrels, shoes, and wagons; blacks who ran away with or acquired a wagon and team operated hack transportation services; others ran fruit stands, laundries, groceries, hotels, and brothels.[36]

A few contrabands began rags-to-riches careers during or just after the war. Like successful immigrants of the time, they often rose by selling groceries and liquor to customers within their ethnic group. Robert R. Church, for example, learned basic business skills as steward on his white father's steamboat. He ran away when Memphis fell to the Federals and started a grocery there with scant resources. Investing profits in other businesses and land, he eventually grew wealthy. However, economic mobility like his rarely occurred; a federal army census in 1865 found that only 3 percent of Memphis black adults were worth $100 or more.[37]

Talent, initiative, perseverance, and luck enabled only a few exceptional contrabands to escape economic dependence. Ironically, the army tried to coerce contrabands into the free labor system; the resulting economic privileges rested tenuously upon the miltary's powerful support and abnormal wartime conditions. Slavery's legacy of exploitation and prejudice remained a serious constraint upon the extent of economic reconstruction.

Wartime Social Reconstruction

Blacks were more successful in winning social privileges because social needs could be fulfilled separately from whites. White Tennesseans remained committed to caste controls, but had little ability to maintain them in garrisoned areas. Paternalistic reformers, like later advocates of Indian reservations, would have preferred to isolate their charges for a controlled introduction to new privileges and responsibilities, but only a minority of Tennessee contrabands entered the camps. These blacks willingly accepted any aid that enhanced freedom, yet always retained their independent-mindedness.

One of their major goals was religious independence. A Chattanooga black told a Northerner that what he wanted most from freedom was an all-black church without white supervision and the right to attend night services without a curfew. During federal occupation, contraband preachers held religious meetings in the open.[38] Urban black chapels began to assert independence from white parent congregations. Two in Nashville switched their affiliation to the African Methodist Episcopal Church and charged that numerous secessionists within the Methodist Church, South, had ruined that denomination's moral integrity.[39]

72

Black churches played an important part in the revision of race relations because of the doctrine of deliverance. The clergy preached that God would help blacks obtain new privileges as part of the providential plan. Moved to action, the churches sponsored schools, and several preachers figured prominently in the black suffrage movement. Throughout, the religious drive remained constructive rather than vindictive. Eaton reported a contraband preacher in Memphis as praying: "O Lord, shake Jeff. Davis ober de mouf ob Hell, but O Lord, doan' drap him in!"[40]

Paternalistic reformers went south presuming that masters permitted slaves to receive little, if any, religious training. They discovered to their surprise that most contrabands, like most Tennessee whites, were Baptists or Methodists.[41] Northern Methodists made no missionary efforts in the state during the war, but the American Baptist Home Mission Society, from the North, ordained black preachers and helped them build congregations. Ministers from other denominations encountered little success in the state and tended to frown upon the preference of contrabands for evangelical religion. Chaplain Joseph Warren, for example, accused them of substituting "feeling for principle, presumption for faith, rant for knowledge, and the noisy demonstrations of occasional religiousness for the daily quiet moralities of life." Except by preaching their moral codes in schools and enforcing it in camps, nonevangelical ministers exerted little influence.[42]

Besides religious independence, contrabands wanted a secure family life. Slave families often ran away as a unit during the war; separated members traveled long distances and took large risks to liberate and reunite relatives.[43] Contraband fathers who enlisted in the federal army showed concern for their families' welfare by sharing rations, moonlighting at odd jobs, or stealing necessities during the long absences of the army paymaster. Because black soldiers' families in Memphis and Nashville lived near federal camps, the men frequently visited them, even when denied permission. An attempt by the Freedmen's Department to force those families in Memphis to move to President's Island ended with the arrival of armed, angry husbands. They and other contrabands showed a commitment to keeping families united.[44]

Believing that a society's soundness depended upon the quality of its family life, paternalistic reformers were concerned that contrabands fulfill familial responsibilities. When Eaton asked his superintendents how slavery had affected the family, he received such answers as "Loose & by example" and "Have had no opportunity for correct notions and practices." Laissez-faire reformer Fiske alone reported that most couples in his camp were faithful to one another and added that "they know what marriage is among the whites." Eaton dismissed such families as exceptions and concluded that most contrabands felt no familial obligations whatsoever. His encounter with a sick contraband's husband illustrates how stubbornly he clung to his preconceptions. Because the husband had purchased a gift not of food or clothing but of candy for his wife, Eaton scolded him for having no sense of duty. In reply, the man angrily recounted the difficulties he had surmounted in locating and freeing his wife, who had been sold away from him before the war. Eaton left offended rather than instructed.[45]

Historians have since demonstrated that close family ties did exist among enslaved blacks. In table 1 only 7 percent of the sample couples willfully ended a marriage. Although firmer unions persevered, shakier marriages often dissolved as slavery deteriorated. The social controls exerted by rural communities were left behind, while the army camps and ghettos presented new temptations. Fights over infidelity frequently led to appearances in police recorder courts.[46] The problematic minority fit the preconceptions of paternalists and thereby captured their attention.

Motivated by moral and practical concerns, reformers often

tried to make contraband marriages successful and secure through legal sanction. Fiske required couples in the Memphis contraband camps to undergo a wedding ritual and used his power as army chaplain to issue marriage certificates, on which American flags were printed to emphasize that the new privilege came from a federal authority. In March 1864 Eaton ordered contrabands who wished to live as couples in the West Tennessee camps to wed; Adjutant General Thomas empowered camp superintendents to conduct the ceremonies. Superintendents instructed applicants in marital duties and enforced those norms within camps. This program, not duplicated elsewhere in Tennessee, fit the paternalistic pattern of combining a new privilege with control and guidance.[47]

The care of parentless children also concerned reformers. When black women began operating orphanages at the President's Island and Clarksville camps, the superintendents placed white women in charge. The institution about which most is known was opened in Memphis by Martha Canfield, a Northern white philanthropist, who tried to provide the best possible environment for the children, including regular attendance at church and school. Relying upon black volunteers recruited by the Reverend Morris Henderson, a black Baptist minister, she wanted their involvement "for their own good . . . [since] they cannot give money, but if encouraged they will give their time, which otherwise might be spent unprofitably." During the first three months of operation, one hundred children entered the orphanage, but only eighteen left, for she was cautious about whom she permitted to be guardians. In Nashville, which lacked an orphanage, poor black families took in most orphans.[48] Although white reformers could better finance orphan care, blacks did not lack a sense of social responsibility, as alleged by the paternalists.

Another area in which contrabands sought advancement was education. Blacks initiated the founding of their first wartime schools in Tennessee. In the fall of 1862 Daniel Wadkins, a free black preacher, surreptitiously started classes in the basement of the First Baptist Church's Colored Mission, in Nashville. At about the same time, in Memphis, contraband employees at an army hospital persuaded Lucinda Humphrey, a white nurse, to hold classes in their quarters at night. Her school, unlike that of Wadkins, was soon discovered by local whites. Because she wanted to continue but did not feel safe in the hospital quarters, she turned the school over to her best pupil, quit nursing, and opened another school in the Shiloh contraband village.[49]

In 1863 Northern freedmen's aid societies began sending teachers into the state and by the war's end had established schools at Memphis, Clarksville, Gallatin, Nashville, Murfreesboro, and Knoxville. To encourage them, contrabands volunteered donations and services, while Adjutant General Thomas provided transportation, rations, and quarters for teachers. In West Tennessee, Eaton made contributions from the freedmen's fund.[50]

Blacks conducted several schools separately from those of Northern societies. Although a few of the teachers were well-educated Northern blacks, most were native Tennesseans who possessed widely varying abilities. A federal officer rated the contraband instructors at Columbia as barely literate but evaluated those at Pulaski as highly competent. In all cases, they needed much dedication. At great personal risk, black teachers opened the first school for contrabands not only at Nashville but also at Columbia, Springfield, and Pulaski. When illness and discouragement caused white teachers to abandon Nashville during the summer of 1864, black teachers continued to hold classes despite harassment from local whites. In 1864 William Jordan received a public whipping at Columbia for teaching fellow slaves in violation of a town ordinance. A commitment to improving their race's status compelled these people to offer their services. Alfred E. Anderson, a free-born

Methodist preacher in Knoxville, taught despite his poor spelling because "I fealt that this pepel must be traind for I knew tha wair humans."[51]

Competition between white and black teachers caused problems. In the fall of 1863 Nelson Merry, black pastor of the First Baptist Colored Mission, in Nashville, permitted the white Reverend Joseph G. McKee to open a free school on the ground floor, thereby challenging Daniel Wadkins, who charged tuition. After the matter sparked an unsightly brawl between Wadkins and Merry, the congregation decided to evict McKee. The black community expected white teachers to respect its instructors and students. Contrabands carefully scrutinized Northerners and openly expressed gratitude or displeasure.[52]

Conflict also occurred among schools of different freedmen's aid societies. Tuition, teacher salary, and equipment varied widely, which added to the grounds for competition over new students and for rivalries among student bodies. Nothing was done about the problem in Middle Tennessee, but in Memphis Adjutant General Thomas empowered Eaton to assume supervision of all schools for contrabands.[53]

Eaton, himself, a school superintendent before the war, wanted to lay the cornerstone of a permanent public education system that was built upon the New England model. He appointed Chaplain Joseph Warren as general superintendent of schools throughout his Freedmen's Department and Chaplain Levi H. Cobb as superintendent for Memphis. Eaton and Cobb standardized tuition, texts, teacher salaries, and procedures. Students who could not afford tuition could pay according to their parents' ability or attend free. Cobb held sole control over allocation of school funds and property, allowing the societies only to audit his accounts.[54]

The new system encountered a succession of difficulties during the fall of 1864. The free black businessmen wanted a separate school for their children, a request Cobb denied. William

C. Hubbard, a white who had profited from unusually high tuitions, refused to bring his school into the system. The superintendent needed to use troops to take possession of the school and dismiss Hubbard. One problem Cobb could not solve was the refusal of many teachers to collect tuition; their view of the schools as charitable institutions angered parents who had to pay. Although rising enrollments prevented a decline in the income of schools, Warren was upset because he wanted to use tuition payments to motivate parents to follow the Work Ethic. Warren and Cobb could not fire noncooperative teachers without damaging the operation of the schools and offending the sponsoring societies. Some teachers and societies grumbled about military interference, but the new system improved educational standards and opportunities for contrabands in Memphis.[55]

The schools sought to build both mental skills and morals. They emphasized the most fundamental skill, reading; devoted secondary, if any, attention to writing and arithmetic; and rarely offered formal classes in subjects beyond the basic three. Some white teachers refrained from holding advanced classes because of their belief that the mentality of blacks was different, though not necessarily inferior. Blacks supposedly were, as Lucinda Humphrey commented, "intuitive and imitative but not reflective."[56] Other obstacles to effective education were overcrowded classes, inadequate facilities, and not enough texts.[57] Still, a number of contrabands gained some basic learning in the new schools.

Illustrating the concern of nineteenth-century education with morals, Eaton charged teachers to "Improve the manners and morals of pupils. Remember that you are for the time the guardians of character and eternal destiny." Besides this common professional attitude, paternalists presumed that slaves had received no moral instruction.[58] Teachers wove Judeo-Christian and Victorian ethics into educational activities. The day often opened or closed with Bible readings, prayers, and hymns. Students used either the old McGuffey's *Eclectic Readers* or the American Tract Society's new *Freedmen's Primer,* both of which stressed cleanliness, politeness, kindness, humility, honesty, thrift, and hard work. The society also published *Freedman*, a newsletter for contraband students which taught that freedom did not include the liberty to sin. Teachers strictly enforced punctuality and order to foster self-discipline; Miss E. A. Otis went to the extreme of beginning each school day with fifteen minutes of silence.[59] *Freedman* and at least a few teachers attempted to shape the students' political values as well as their morals. Miss Humphrey, for example, lectured on "liberty and slavery, the President's Proclamation, the war."[60]

According to nineteenth-century thought, the development of skills and character made education a key to self-advancement. When contrabands learned to read, write, or calculate, they gained tools that helped them cope more effectively with the world and occasionally to improve their personal fortunes. The impact of the moral and political lessons is not so clear. Undoubtedly, as Eaton noted, "whatever education has been accomplished among the people cannot be taken from them."[61]

The privilege of education also improved social status. Startled by the sight of black children carrying schoolbooks, a new member of the Pulaski camp exclaimed: "Lord a massy! Gwine to school like white folks!" This change offended many whites, like the woman who scolded the Reverend McKee: "The time was when the niggers carried the white children's books and dinner and waited outside to bring them home. Now we have no schools and these Yankees are opening free schools for niggers."[62] When one Nashville mistress caught a slave studying a speller, she grabbed it and threw it in the fire. Another owner drove a slave out of his home in midwinter because she had sent her children to school. Civilians, though, could not effectively combat the education of contrabands in schools protected by the army. Angry whites closed only two schools during the war, one with threats and the other with arson.[63]

During the course of federal occupation, Tennessee contrabands gained religious independence, familial security, and educational opportunities. They could take advantage of wartime social disruptions to liberate their family and religion from white interference, but only Northern reformers possessed the power to obtain marriage licenses and numerous schools for them. Although not improving the material conditions of life, the new social privileges significantly increased the control of contrabands over their private lives, which reflected and partly fulfilled their sense of human dignity. They expressed gratitude for the help of reformers, but the latter showed little appreciation for the independent efforts of blacks to reconstruct their social and economic position. Only after a year's experience working with contrabands did William F. Mitchell of the Pennsylvania Freedmen's Relief Association write: "I have . . . heretofore pleaded for the Freedmen, for what *they can be made* under the influence of freedom. Hereafter I contend for the colored people of Tennessee for what they *are.*"[64]

6

Black Military Service

During the spring of 1863 Lorenzo Thomas traveled the length of the Mississippi Valley addressing federal troops about the army's manpower shortage and the expediency of recruiting as many contrabands as possible to fill the gap. Congress had empowered Lincoln to accept black recruits in July 1862, but he showed little interest in the idea until he issued the Final Emancipation Proclamation. Then, under orders from Stanton, the adjutant general inaugurated a massive enlistment program in the Western war theater. Thomas's great authority and rousing oratory dampened dissent in the ranks, and a number of post commanders enthusiastically began recruiting black regiments. Slaves, whom Tennessee law had prohibited from bearing arms, now gained their ultimate opportunity for contributing to slavery's destruction. The number of contrabands and their extensive use by Federals significantly helped the eventual Union triumph.[1]

Even before recruiting commenced, contrabands had offered to fight. During Confederate attacks on Nashville in late 1862 and on Fort Donelson early the next year, federal commanders refused these offers. At Fort Donelson the contrabands disregarded orders, picked up rifles from wounded soldiers, and joined the action.[2]

When Thomas arrived in West Tennessee, he found that the

81

volunteer guards at the contraband camps wanted to enlist. Eaton and other paternalists, believing that military service would foster manly qualities, also favored enlistment. Brigadier General Nathan Kimball, post commander at Jackson, was so strongly interested in the idea that he had begun recruiting an unauthorized regiment, the first in the state. Thomas officially approved this action and empowered Eaton's subordinates to recruit within contraband camps.[3] Supported by Grant, Thomas started additional efforts at Bolivar, La Grange, and Memphis.[4]

Initiating black recruitment in Middle Tennessee was not so easy in view of Military Governor Johnson's opposition. Because of prejudice, he disliked raising the status of blacks from laborers to soldiers and, knowing that other whites felt likewise, he feared it would harm the Union cause in Tennessee. In March 1863 Lincoln fruitlessly urged Johnson to recruit blacks. On the Fourth of July, Private James T. Ayers, from Illinois, obtained General Eleazer A. Paine's permission to begin recruiting and training contrabands at Gallatin. The general nervously telegraphed Johnson four times in thirteen days and begged for the necessary authorization. Frustrated by the lack of response, Paine finally shipped the recruits to Nashville by train. Upon their arrival, Johnson agreed to muster them in— his first black enlistees. Several days later, under pressure from Lorenzo Thomas, General Rosecrans began a recruiting program, which in actuality only enlisted impressed laborers into noncombat regiments.[5]

In late August, Stanton assigned Major George L. Stearns to direct and expand black recruitment in Middle Tennessee. This militant abolitionist, one of the financiers of John Brown's raid on Harper's Ferry, came to Nashville "determined to burn slavery out, or be burned by it myself." The appointment must have appalled Johnson, who, like other Southern politicians in 1859, had vehemently condemned Brown's conspiracy. Johnson had publicly endorsed emancipation only a few days before Stearns arrived and still strongly preferred Rosecrans's limited program.[6]

On September 16 Johnson told Stearns he would object to any large-scale recruiting effort and wired Washington the next day to request the major's removal, charging that "his notions" would offend the public. Lincoln's reply yielded nothing: "Let me urge that you do your utmost to get every man you can, black and white, under arms at the earliest moment." Stanton's accompanying note reaffirmed the new policy of black enlistment, but conceded that "if Major Stearns . . . is obnoxious, he will of course be removed." Johnson bowed to the administration's wishes and decided to coexist with Stearns. Yet, before recruiting began, the military governor obtained a promise that the War Department would pay unionist slaveholders $300 for each slave manumitted and enlisted. Stearns then established a wide network of recruiting stations, at Fort Donelson, Clarksville, Gallatin, Nashville, Murfreesboro, McMinnville, Columbia, Wartrace, Shelbyville, Lynnville, Pulaski, Pikeville, and Chattanooga.[7]

During the winter of 1863–64 the black recruitment structure in Tennessee was reorganized under the leadership of Brigadier General Augustus L. Chetlain, based in Memphis. In Nashville, Stearns resigned because of personal differences with Stanton. Colonel Mussey, Stearns's assistant, received command over recruiting in Middle and East Tennessee, including a new operation at Knoxville.[8] Although both Chetlain and Mussey were Midwestern radical Republicans, they demonstrated their devotion to emancipation differently. Chetlain, a former businessman, concentrated on efficient recruiting and studiously avoided publicity. Mussey, a former journalist, frequently entered the public spotlight and also cultivated good relations with Johnson in order to champion the interests of the contrabands.[9]

Recruiters faced obstacles in obtaining large-scale enlistments. One black soldier observed that a "heap of slaves was afraid to go [in] to the army." Enlistment was the ultimate act of treason against Southern white society, and the potential recruit had every reason to fear harsh retaliation. A married contraband might refrain from joining the army out of concern for his family's welfare and safety in his absence, especially if they remained with a master. During the early part of the war, the black private earned only $10 a month (minus the cost of clothes), and civilian employment paid much more.[10] The contraband enlistee also lost much of his newly won independence by entering another white-controlled, authoritarian institution.

Recruiters consequently devised means for enticing volunteers, often by appealing to patriotism and racial pride. The officers sought to allay the family man's anxieties by providing for dependents' needs within a contraband camp and sometimes by aiding the wife to find a job.[11] Because of the low pay, recruiters concentrated on recent runaways, as Eaton put it, "before their minds have been corrupted by life at private service, or in cities." During the summer of 1864 Congress helped by raising the black private's monthly pay to $16 and by granting an enlistment bounty of $300.[12]

Stearns and Mussey used black recruiters effectively and sent individual agents into the countryside, even behind Confederate lines. Marching black troops through rural areas brought the most success because their sudden appearance, en masse, uniformed, organized, and armed, deeply impressed slaves who lived in rustic isolation. A White County field hand later recalled: "They came right in my house, I walked out with them, never said a God's word to nobody." Taking pride in his self-emancipation and his new associates, he, of course, joined the regiment.[13]

Black leaders in Memphis and Nashville argued that only

direct military action would end slavery. Referring to the doctrine of deliverance, one declared: "God will rule over our destinies . . . [which are those of] a people bursting their bonds and rallying for freedom. (Applause) To do this, and to maintain in the future our liberties when won, we must learn to use arms; we must be a fighting people." Another speaker added: "Why don't you remember how afraid they used to be that we would rise? And you know we would, too, if we could (Cries of 'That's so')."[14] The time had come when many slaves could and did rebel in the controlled form of military service.

The risks and sacrifices involved in this restricted enlistments. Possibly inspired by passage of the Conscription Act, several post commanders in West Tennessee began forcing unemployed contrabands into the army during the summer of 1863. Thomas and Grant soon endorsed the practice, but they acted by military fiat because the law never applied to occupied Confederate states.[15] In early 1864 recruiters extended conscription to East Tennessee, but General Sherman, who disliked black troops, halted involuntary enlistments in West Tennessee. When Sherman succeeded Grant as commander of the Military Division of the Mississippi, Chetlain quietly resumed conscription, apparently realizing his superior would be too busy to notice.[16] Chetlain's patrols grew aggressive enough to interfere with the contract labor system and seize a number of employed blacks, disregarding their passes. The ugly practice continued through the war in West and East Tennessee, despite a high desertion rate among conscripts.[17]

In Middle Tennessee, Stearns accepted only voluntary enlistments because of his laissez-faire beliefs. As soon as he left the state, several recruiters began conscripting blacks in order to increase the monetary commissions they received per head. Before Mussey could react, Adjutant General Thomas ordered him to enlist every able-bodied black man.[18] Large-scale conscription quickly angered masters, employers, and proslavery

85

Federals. The post commander at La Vergne arrested a white captain and his black troops for forcing slaves into the army. After their release, the captain obstinately led a second expedition into the same neighborhood, and this time General Rousseau had him imprisoned. Rousseau also discharged a group of contraband conscripts who had worked in a federal woodyard at Wartrace. The Springfield post commander appealed to Johnson to make recruiters relinquish conscripted slaves, but, when the order arrived, nearly all volunteered to enlist.[19]

The controversy culminated when complaints reached Grant about conscription of an entire repair crew from the militarily controlled Tennessee and Alabama Railroad. Grant, then heading the Military Division of the Mississippi, instantly requested the adjutant general to return the men. Fearing the powerful commander's displeasure, Thomas swiftly absolved himself by ordering the laborers released and by revoking his conscription order for Middle Tennessee "as recruiting officers have shown no discretion." In March 1864 Grant issued an order forbidding conscription of contraband laborers, and Rousseau prohibited the forced enlistment of any black on the grounds that it deprived slaveholders of their means of support.[20]

Colonel Mussey obeyed the new orders but yearned to demolish slavery by enlisting every able-bodied black man, something other recruiters were then attempting in Kentucky. Contradicting his usual laissez-faire stance, he advocated the extension of the Conscription Act to Tennessee. Military Governor Johnson ordered all able-bodied men of military age enrolled in the state militia, but, to Mussey's disappointment, he neither called them into service nor asked for a federal draft quota. Except in Memphis and Chattanooga, where local commanders temporarily activated the militia, enrollment amounted merely to writing names on forms.[21]

Black enlistment aroused much controversy in Tennessee,

but white civilians could do little to resist it beyond punishing soldiers' families or inducing enlistees to desert. East Tennessee unionists, on the other hand, used their political influence to limit the recruiting in their region.[22] The most effective opposition came from within the army, beginning with several post commanders who tried to block the enlistment of their laborers. In June 1864 General Sherman, infuriated by the constant reduction of contraband crews during his momentous campaign against Atlanta, forbade the recruitment of employed blacks throughout the Military Division of the Mississippi. Protests by Mussey and Adjutant General Thomas failed to lift the ban. General George H. Thomas held Mussey under arrest for nearly two weeks until the colonel apologized for his criticism.[23]

Adamantly opposed to any increase in black enlistments, Sherman also fought an 1864 law that amended the Conscription Act to permit Northern states to fill their quotas by recruiting blacks in certain occupied areas. The act did not allow state agents to recruit in Tennessee, but, when Sherman denied them access to military transportation and rations below Nashville and Memphis, he sorely tempted them to break the law.[24] The agents, considered "mere Sharpers . . . men buyers" by Mussey, began recruiting Tennessee blacks, enticing those already enlisted to desert for reenlistment under them and bribing federal officers to aid their corrupt practices. To halt recruiting abuses, Mussey required that mustering officers investigate the background of these recruits before accepting them. Fortunately, in early 1865 Congress repealed the problematic law.[25]

When wartime recruitment of blacks ended on June 1, 1865, a total of 20,133 had enlisted in Tennessee. Congress had decreed the year before that slaves would receive their freedom upon being mustered into the army. Because some enlistees came from other states, the total figure reveals only that something less than 39 percent of the state's male slaves of military age gained legal freedom in this way. Still, that percentage was much larger than the 20 percent of white male Tennesseans of military age who joined the federal army.[26]

White officers in black regiments regarded military service as a way of training freedmen for a new place in society. Like the contraband camps and the contract labor system, the regiments were paternalistic institutions. The federal hierarchy not only provided for the black enlistee's subsistence but also tried to guide and control his life. Although this was true for white recruits too, many officers believed that blacks needed more help. The army began by changing their personal appearance. It sheared hair, burned slave clothes, provided thorough washings, and furnished new uniforms.

The fledgling soldier then entered military training, which, according to Colonel Robert Cowden, of the 59th U.S. Colored Infantry, was designed to transform him: "All that he has ever learned except prompt, unquestioning obedience must be unlearned. The plantation manners, the awkward bowing and scraping at two or three rods distance, with hat under arm, and with averted look, must be exchanged for the upright form, the open face, the gentlemanly address and soldierly salute." Then as today, the army built up the morale of enlistees by stimulating their pride in marksmanship, military appearance, and drilling skills. The goal of the entire process, in an officer's words, was "to cultivate in them self-respect and all manly qualities."[27]

The officers regarded high standards of conduct as essential in fortifying the character of black soldiers and in winning public respect for them. Military records reveal a strong effort to maintain strict discipline. A few officers, including a colonel who flogged miscreants, went to extremes, but army discipline was usually neither as arbitrary nor as severe as that in slavery. A private in the 13th U.S. Colored Infantry observed: "Our old masters would get angry with us and sometimes punish us almost to death, and we not understand why; but here if we are punished, we know why for the officers tell us our duty and never punish us unless we disobey."[28]

Because the soldiers had lived under slavery did not mean, as some historians suggest, that they had become thoroughly subservient to or dependent upon authority figures.[29] Slaves often acquired a serenely deceptive character, which contributed to major disciplinary problems in some of the regiments. Blacks readily absorbed from white Federals the attitude that Southern civilians enjoyed no rights that need be respected; those caught in depredations fell back on servile language in trying to elicit a merciful reaction. In Memphis the nearby presence of their families caused continual problems: the men preferred to spend nights with their wives rather than in camp and they stole government supplies to help provide for their dependents.[30] A company of the 13th U. S. Colored Infantry, at Johnsonville, mutinied after Rousseau prohibited the troops from leaving camp. Some black artillerymen in Memphis mutinied when one of them was punished in a way they considered to be extreme and uncustomary. Throughout the war, discipline remained a major concern of the white officers.[31]

Some of them went beyond military training and discipline in their efforts to prepare the men for a free life. Many encouraged thrift by starting company banks. Colonel Cowden held discussions with his men about the dangers of idleness and the rewards of industry.[32] In at least half of the Tennessee black regiments, chaplains or company officers taught classes; dedicated students kept their texts on hand for study during spare moments, even when on picket or labor assignments. Officers encouraged men to read newspapers and in at least one case assigned company paperwork to a black sergeant as soon as he was literate enough.[33] Former slaves who left the army with an education and savings had indeed made tangible gains.

Military service could produce a deep psychological impact on the slave volunteer. From the perspective of his old age, a sergeant realized that "This was the biggest thing that ever happened in my life. I felt like a man with a uniform on and a gun in my hand." The self-esteem that flowed from belonging to a powerful army increased the sense of importance. Conducting a former master under military arrest to the Clarksville jail, a soldier boasted: "Massa, you put this nigger in dar two or free years ago—now dis nigga put you in dar, massa, yah, yah, yah."[34] Armed with new privileges and power, the black soldier awaited a reevaluation of his social status.

Most whites, however, reacted to him with hostility. Confederate sympathizers, of course, viewed enlisted contrabands as traitors to the South. Belle Edmondson, a teenage secessionist, prayed that "God grant not one life of our dear Soldiers will be sacrificed to those cowardly dogs." Critics argued that armed slaves lacked the courage needed to fight Confederates, but would readily slaughter helpless civilians. The first time a black regiment camped in one Memphis neighborhood, terrified residents kept their homes lit all night. After failing to convince the post commander to place white guards around their homes, they were surprised to find that the unit behaved better than most of its white predecessors.[35]

Prejudiced whites deeply resented the transformation of powerless slaves into agents of federal military might.[36] Feeling humiliated, a woman in Gallatin protested that "I will die on the pavement and rot there before *I* will ask a 'nigger' to let *me* pass." Nashville civilians began to respect black sentries only after one of them shot a white who had deliberately disobeyed a warning and crossed a picket line without authorization. The black troops endured much verbal harassment and a few assaults.[37]

Some white unionists and Federals responded positively to black soldiers because of hatred for the enemy. One white private wrote home: "There is not a Negro in the army . . . for whom I have not a thousand times more respect than I have for a traitor to his country. . . . No traitor is too good to be killed by a Negro."[38] The service of black troops sometimes moved Federals and unionists to modify their prejudices. Another Union soldier reminisced: "This readiness of the negroes to become soldiers exalted their manhood in the estimation of the Union soldiers, for . . . the volunteer soldier's great and final test of manhood was bravery to face the enemy."[39]

Bravery, as is well known, never won blacks equal treatment from the army bureaucracy. No Tennesseans of that race served as commissioned officers except for two lieutenants in the enrolled militia at Memphis; most West Tennessee regiments did not even have black sergeants.[40] Army hospitals refused to treat sick or wounded blacks lest the races mix under the same roof. At first, blacks could receive medical care only in the sick quarters of their regiments or in a contraband hospital, but Adjutant General Thomas eventually convinced military authorities in Memphis and Nashville to establish separate hospitals for them.[41] The army originally paid blacks $10 a month (minus the cost of clothes) regardless of rank, but the pay of noncommissioned whites ran from $13 for privates to $21 for sergeants. Whites also received a federal enlistment bounty. Black troops throughout the occupied South resented this discrimination, and some, including a brigade at Chattanooga, protested by refusing to accept any pay. In June 1864 Congress remedied the inequity by granting black soldiers the same compensation scale and bounty as whites.[42]

Possibly the most significant inequity was the disproportionate assignment of black troops to fatigue and guard duty. When recruiting diminished the supply of contraband military laborers, commanders simply assigned black troops to do the work. Several regiments, made up of men unfit for field service, were enlisted specifically for noncombat duties. In other units, overly frequent labor assignments seriously reduced time for military training and led to disciplinary problems.[43] During 1864 Adjutant General Thomas, who had originally planned to place blacks exclusively in rear-area garrisons, joined Chetlain and Mussey in favoring their use in combat. Racial biases of both William T. Sherman and George H. Thomas continued to limit field assignments. Thomas Cole, stationed at Chattanooga, later recalled his feelings: "when dey wents to battle I was always left in camp ter helps take care of de supplies. General Thomas calls me a coward."[44]

Confederate attacks on Tennessee posts inaugurated the black troops into combat. First blood was drawn in December 1863, at Moscow, where the 61st U.S. Colored Infantry participated in a skirmish that successfully defended the railroad depot there.[45] Next came a major battle at Fort Pillow on April 12, 1864. After Confederate forces under Major General Nathan B. Forrest, a former slave trader from Memphis, defeated the racially mixed garrison, a massacre took place.

Confederates inevitably viewed the federal decision to enlist blacks as a provocation for slave rebellion. The Confederate government never officially acknowledged black Federals as soldiers but allowed them to be treated either as property to be restored to owners or as insurrectionaries to be executed. The law left the disposition of captured black Federals up to state authorities, which for all practical purposes no longer existed in Tennessee.[46]

Prior to Fort Pillow, Confederates had fought black troops only a few times. Forrest himself had first encountered them a short time earlier at Paducah, Kentucky, where he tried in vain to force the racially mixed garrison to surrender by threatening to grant no quarter if it fought. After his attack failed, he moved southward. In the subsequent Fort Pillow battle, he used units of his command that had stayed behind in Tennessee and had never confronted black soldiers.[47]

Portions of the 13th Tennessee Cavalry, 6th U.S. Colored Heavy Artillery, and 2d U.S. Colored Light Artillery, mostly raw recruits, made up the fort's garrison. About half the men were black. Forrest led veteran units that were two-and-a-half times the size of the adversary force. After several hours of combat, he sent a surrender demand to the fort under a flag of truce. He promised the entire garrison all consideration due prisoners of war and, unlike his Paducah ultimatum, did not threaten them with no quarter if they continued fighting. The Federals refused to surrender, and some blacks tauntingly threatened to give the Confederates no quarter. This further inflamed the enemy because, as a Confederate journalist reported, "the sight of negro troops stirred the bosoms of our soldiers with courageous madness." The next charge smashed into the fort. The Federals made a brief but determined stand, then fled down a nearly perpendicular bluff, only to find themselves trapped against the Mississippi River by surrounding Confederates.[48]

Defenders of the Confederates have argued that the Federals were drunk and that they kept up a senseless last-ditch resistance. The first charge is suspect, not only because it is a common propagandist device, but also because it did not appear until after the incident gained public notoriety.[49] A report, written by Forrest in self-defense, claimed only that the Federals kept up an organized resistance as they retreated down the bluff. No federal statement made immediately after the battle mentioned this, and the 2d U.S. Colored Light Artillery's report said instead that the post commander ordered every man to save himself when the Confederates came over the fort's embankment.[50] If some Federals continued to fight, the cause was the refusal of many Confederates to take prisoners.

Confederate surgeon Samuel H. Caldwell described the scene in a letter to his wife: "Terrible was the slaughter—it was decidedly the most horrible sight that I have ever witnessed." Confederate Sergeant Achilles V. Clark wrote home that "the poor deluded negroes would run up to our men fall upon their knees and with uplifted hands scream for mercy but they were ordered to their feet and then shot down."[51] Military records indicate that about half the garrison died, but that, though no more than 34 percent of the white troops were killed, the black units suffered a death toll of 64 percent (see table 6).[52] As a Confederate newspaper reported, "The whites received quarter, but the negroes were shown no mercy." Many Confederates in this initial encounter refused to recognize black Federals as anything but rebel slaves who deserved summary punishment.[53]

Table 6. Federal Casualties at Fort Pillow

	White Units[a]	Black Units	Total
Killed/missing[b]	65–83	185	250–268
Died from wounds	21	10	31
Total dead	86–104	195	281–299
Percentage dead	31–34%	64%	48–49%
Captured	151	51	202
Escaped	8	29	37
Wounded and sick survivors	39	30	69
Total survivors	198	110	308
Grand Total	284–302	305	589–607

[a]This column includes three men on detached duty from Illinois, Kansas, and Missouri regiments.

[b]Relatively few Compiled Service Records state that soldiers were definitely killed. The records on blacks presume that all missing men were killed, and this table follows that guideline. The only alternative, an unlikely one, would have been for a survivor to escape and desert. Otherwise, these are conservative figures because each unit may have had additional unmustered men serving with it who died without leaving any military records.

Some Confederates accepted and protected surrendering Federals. A handful of officers attempted to restore discipline in the ranks. Sergeant Clark commented: "I with several others tried to stop the butchery and at one time had partially succeeded—but Gen. Forrest ordered them shot down like dogs—and the carnage continued." Several federal survivors remembered hearing Confederates say that Forrest had ordered the killing of the blacks. No direct evidence that he did so has been found; even Clark did not claim to have heard Forrest give the order. Wrathful officers, acting in the heat of the moment, might have used Forrest's name without authorization. If he did order a massacre, he quickly changed his mind; he and Brigadier General James R. Chalmers, the officer who was second in command, personally stopped the killing. Surgeon Caldwell believed that "if General Forrest had not run between our men & the Yanks with his Pistol and sabre drawn not a man would have been spared."[54] Obviously, resistance had ended by that time or the generals would not have exposed themselves.

Neither of the two expressed regret about the incident. Federal naval officers, who spoke to Chalmers under a flag of truce after the battle, reported him as saying "it was nothing better than we could expect so long as we persisted in arming the negro." Forrest gloated over the federal casualties in his battle report: "The river was dyed with the blood of the slaughtered for 200 yards. . . . It is hoped that these facts will demonstrate to the Northern people that negro soldiers cannot cope with Southerners."[55]

Forrest took his black prisoners into Mississippi, where he treated them as recaptured property. The remnant of the 6th U.S. Colored Heavy Artillery publicly swore to revenge the unit, and several black regiments adopted "Remember Fort Pillow" as a battle cry. In a report intended for use as war propaganda, the federal congressional Committee on the Conduct of the War charged Forrest's army with atrociously massacring the Fort Pillow garrison. The intensity of the controversy and possibly fear of retaliation not only prompted Forrest to disclaim any guilt but also probably prevented similar incidents. Through the rest of the war, Confederates usually treated black military prisoners as recaptured property rather than as insurrectionaries.[56]

The 6th U.S. Colored Heavy Artillery did not obtain its revenge, and black troops saw practically no more action in West Tennessee during the war. In Middle Tennessee, a series of Confederate raids finally brought black regiments into combat during the fall of 1864. The 14th U.S. Colored Infantry beat off Forrest's cavalry in a skirmish at Pulaski. Forrest took a supply depot at Johnsonville from the 12th U.S. Colored Infantry, but the regiment evaded capture. Most of the 11th U.S. Colored Infantry became his prisoners when he took a string of blockhouses they had manned along the Tennessee and Alabama Railroad. General Hood captured the entire 44th U.S. Colored Infantry in Georgia and took its troops along as military laborers during his invasion of Tennessee, but 300 escaped, reformed, and fought their way to Nashville.[57]

Before the climactic Battle of Nashville, on December 15–16, 1864, General George H. Thomas had never used black troops in combat, but, as Hood's army swept forward, he was compelled to concentrate all available units in the city's defenses. On the first day of battle, he ordered the 12th, 13th, 14th, 17th, 18th, and 44th U.S. Colored Infantries to feign an attack against Hood's right wing. Their success in diverting Confederate attention enabled Thomas to deliver a smashing blow against Hood's left wing. The Confederates then retreated to higher ground and formed new defensive lines.[58]

On the second day of fighting, the black regiments joined an attack on Hood's well-fortified center. The first charge failed despite heavy casualties but sufficiently preoccupied the enemy so that the federal right wing could again crash through the Confederate left. Shouts of victory coming from the other side of the battlefield emboldened the federal center to overrun the opponents with a second charge, which completed the rout of Hood's army. As Thomas watched the final assault from afar, he underwent a change of heart and declared to his staff, "the question is settled; the negroes will fight." They also realized they had proven their worth. Catching sight of Thomas as they marched from the field, they fell into a precise drill formation and passed singing the militant abolitionist song "John Brown's Body."[59]

The privilege of bearing arms changed the position of former slaves in society. Strengthened by a sense of personal dignity, black veterans would not readily submit to subjection again, nor could the federal government conscientiously permit their reenslavement. By risking their lives for their country, they had laid a claim to freedom and greater rights for their race after the war.

7

The Politics of Emancipation

Although contrabands had gained virtual freedom, only white politicians could make it legal. Northern Republicans and their Southern unionist allies originally waged war just to save the Union. Growing numbers of contrabands and their many services pressured the politicians to broaden war aims. The federal government's eventual decision to do so forced many reluctant unionists to abandon an institution with which they had always lived.

After secession in 1861, Southern unionists had nowhere to turn but to the Republicans who controlled the federal government. During that summer, Senator Andrew Johnson and Kentucky Congressman John J. Crittenden induced the Republican majority in Congress to pass resolutions renouncing abolition as a possible war aim, thereby encouraging cooperation with Southern unionists.[1] Johnson's subsequent appointment as military governor made him the key intermediary between Tennessee unionists and the administration.

Federal invasion of the state in 1862 enabled unionists to return home, where they soon chafed under military governance. Realizing that successful restoration of civilian rule depended upon expansion of unionist support, Johnson led a campaign to restore public allegiance to the federal government. As they had done during the secession referendum, unionists denied that Northerners intended to destroy slavery and pointed for proof to the congressional war aim resolutions and the army's exclusion of runaways. To intensify their impact, Johnson and his associates threatened to support emancipation should continued rebellion force them to choose between slavery and the Union.[2]

Increasing slave disloyalty and changing federal policies embarrassed the unionists. This group tried to excuse the army's impressment of slave laborers and nonenforcement of the Fugitive Slave Law as unavoidable consequences of an efficient prosecution of the war. Secessionists, they asserted, were more responsible for damage suffered by slavery because secession had caused the war and federal occupation. During most of 1862 unionists expected to salvage slavery after a quick defeat of the Confederacy.[3]

During 1862–63 Tennessee's two congressmen tried to restrain federal encroachments upon slavery. Horace Maynard and Andrew J. Clements voted against the new article of war prohibiting military enforcement of the Fugitive Slave Law. Both fought the Second Confiscation Act, but Maynard joined the Republican majority during the final vote.[4] This division illustrated the dilemma southern unionists faced because numerical weakness limited their influence on federal policy while making their safety dependent upon federal troops. When the national government adopted distasteful policies, unionists were forced to choose from three unpleasant alternatives: they could switch their allegiance to the enemy, a step few combat-hardened unionists could stomach; they could dissent, an action that might damage the unity and effectiveness of the war effort; or they could submit, the painful and humiliating choice that alone would satisfy their powerful allies.

If emancipation had to happen, then both congressmen favored a program that Lincoln had proposed to the border states. Under the plan, the states would pass gradual emancipation laws, and the federal government would help states compensate slaveholders. Because the two congressmen considered emancipation harmful to society, they demanded that the federal government colonize any slaves who were freed.[5]

The increasingly strained relationship between Tennessee unionists and the Republican administration reached a critical point in September 1862, when Lincoln's Preliminary Emancipation Proclamation threatened to free all slaves in the state. Because of it, Thomas A. R. Nelson, the most prominent unionist behind Confederate lines in East Tennessee, converted to the rebel side. In a widely circulated address, he condemned the proclamation as an act of "despotism . . . atrocity and barbarism." Confederates won only a few such converts, but the possibility of significant enemy gains terrified unionist leaders who were behind federal lines. The Memphis *Bulletin* denounced the proclamation as "unconstitutional and inexpedient, and calculated to crucify the Union men of the Border States."[6]

Because it included an escape clause, the proclamation did not immediately force displeased unionists to choose between opposition and submission. The president promised to exempt any area that renewed its allegiance to the federal government by sending representatives to Congress before January 1, 1863. Through the threat of emancipation, Lincoln sought to restore at least the semblance of loyalty in federally occupied areas, the only places where congressional elections could conceivably occur. He urged Johnson to hold elections so that Tennesseans could "avoid the unsatisfactory prospect before them." A year earlier, after Confederate congressional elections, unionist winners in the four easternmost districts had attempted to join the federal Congress instead; only Maynard and Clements had reached Washington.[7] Now that much of West and Middle Tennessee lay behind federal lines, Tennessee potentially could produce a nearly complete delegation by January.

Fearing secessionist candidates would win, the military governor did not want to risk elections. Unionists in West Tennessee, the region where the slave proportion was the largest, repeatedly petitioned him to issue writs of election; by late November, those in the upper counties became desperate enough to plan an extralegal balloting. At the last minute, Johnson called a congressional election for December 29 in just the two West Tennessee districts.[8]

At about the time the writs appeared, William B. Campbell, a former governor and a leading Middle Tennessee unionist, approached Johnson with another scheme for preventing emancipation in the state. Campbell proposed that unionist leaders petition Lincoln to exempt Tennessee on grounds that Confederate raiders would prevent the allegedly loyal majority from holding a fair election. The military governor placed his all-important signature on the petition alongside forty others. William G. Brownlow and Congressman Maynard, neither being in Tennessee at the time, independently notified Lincoln of their support for the state's exemption. Emerson Etheridge, a prominent West Tennessean, presented Campbell's petition to the president on December 23.[9]

Meanwhile, congressional campaigns had been progressing in West Tennessee, where at least two of the final four candidates ran on platforms condemning emancipation. A unionist convention at Bolivar passed resolutions instructing the district's victor to vote against emancipation measures and for tougher fugitive slave laws. Lincoln's proclamation had indeed aroused interest in the election, but of a variety hostile to his policies. The administration escaped further embarrassment when a Confederate raid actually did prevent voting. By then, the election had become irrelevant, for Campbell's petition had swayed Lincoln to exempt Tennessee from the Final Emancipation Proclamation.[10]

Although they had prevented emancipation in Tennessee,

unionists found themselves in an anomalous position. Could they continue to support an administration that had declared slaves in most other Southern states free without eventually accepting emancipation in their own state? Like unionists in other exempted areas (parts of Virginia and Louisiana), they began to divide. Etheridge and Campbell led a faction that denounced Lincoln for his emancipation policy; Brownlow headed a group that dropped proslavery commitments and declared unconditional support for the administration. The rest neither criticized Lincoln nor gave emancipation an unqualified endorsement; Johnson and Maynard continued to make rhetorical threats about favoring emancipation if rebellion did not end soon. In an 1863 Fourth of July oration, published for mass distribution, Maynard even promised the reenslavement of contrabands if support for the Confederacy would cease.[11]

As Kentucky, Maryland, and Delaware had already demonstrated, the best protection against federal interference with slavery was a unionist state government. Opponents of the administration demanded the holding of a gubernatorial and legislative election in August 1863, as scheduled by the state constitution. When Johnson refused to terminate his military government that soon, dissidents held an extralegal gubernatorial canvass in several counties. They proclaimed Campbell the winner, but Lincoln's refusal to recognize the election ended the matter.[12]

The gubernatorial controversy pointedly demonstrated Johnson's power and influence. Once he took sides, he clearly would play a key role in enacting or resisting emancipation. He had helped win Tennessee's exemption from the Final Emancipation Proclamation, but during 1863 the Lincoln administration grew more insistent upon border state emancipation.[13] Unyielding opposition could result in Johnson's loss of the military governorship.

The Politics of Emancipation

During an impromptu speech on August 29, 1863, Johnson finally declared himself in favor of immediate emancipation. His intense class consciousness (a byproduct of his difficult rise from poverty), his Jacksonian belief in equal opportunities for white men, and his political ambitions eased his acceptance of emancipation. In line with his 1861 charge that secessionists would create an autocracy ruled by slaveholders, his central argument ran: "The slave aristocracy had long held their foot upon their necks, and exacted heavy tribute from them, even to robbing them of free speech. Let the era of freedom henceforth be proclaimed to the non-slaveholders of Tennessee!"[14]

Johnson's advocacy of immediate emancipation, at a time when Lincoln had only been asking for gradual emancipation in border states, was not as significant as it appeared because he wanted enactment through legislative action. The legislature would need to pass a proposed constitutional amendment in two consecutive general assemblies and then hold a popular referendum on it. Once a legislature had been elected, the process would take at least two years. Johnson also hoped that the legislature would pass a black code, which would place some restrictions on the freedmen.[15]

Shortly after Johnson's public conversion, Major George L. Stearns arrived in Nashville. Besides beginning black recruitment, he tried to talk unionist leaders into some sort of quick emancipation scheme, probably involving a petition to Lincoln for withdrawal of Tennessee's exemption from the Final Emancipation Proclamation. Johnson was too much of a states' rights Democrat to sanction such a plan. Furthermore, he received a letter from Lincoln urging the rapid accomplishment of emancipation and reconstruction through state constitutional revision. This would require Johnson to change his plans, but in a more acceptable way than Stearns's scheme. The major's intrusion into Tennessee politics no doubt contributed to Johnson's abortive attempt to have him removed.[16]

103

More than two hundred Middle Tennessee unionists, led by the Reverend John W. Bowen, decided to send the president a petition, but it only condemned slavery and called for the equal payment of black troops. Johnson did not sign it, though Manson M. Brien and other close allies did. The growing body of antislavery unionists became restless and called mass meetings in an effort to nudge the military governor to act on emancipation. [17]

Although blacks enjoyed no political rights in Tennessee, they did not watch passively as white politicians debated slavery's fate. Ignoring prohibitory laws, they held mass meetings in Nashville and Memphis. At the first of these, on the Fourth of July 1863, in Nashville a slave read the Declaration of Independence and commented upon his race's equal right to liberty. A gathering of Memphis blacks on the first anniversary of the Final Emancipation Proclamation based demands for freedom and new privileges upon a sense of human dignity underlined by a resolution on self-respect: "We are highly gratified by the appellation by which the colored soldiers are addressed by their officers, viz.: *men*; and we urge the colored men in all places, at all times, and under all circumstances to cease using that vulgar phrase, 'nigger.'" [18]

Urban blacks began holding marches that were often led by black regiments and for which black businessmen served as parade marshals. Ministers, military employees, benevolent societies, craftsmen, and schoolchildren walked as units under banners and transparencies bearing slogans like "Liberty or Death" and "Free and Equal." Marches usually occurred in celebration of some special event, such as anniversaries of the Final Emancipation Proclamation or emancipation in the British West Indies. [19]

Pressured by blacks, antislavery unionists, and Lincoln, Johnson finally unveiled a new emancipation plan on January 21, 1864. By this time, the federal army had cleared Confederates from all but the northeastern corner of Tennessee and thus opened the way for statewide reconstruction. In an obviously staged maneuver at a mass meeting of Nashville unionists, a resolutions committee proposed that the military governor begin reconstruction with a state constitutional convention, which should propose an amendment for immediate emancipation. Because Tennessee's constitution did not explicitly provide for constitutional conventions, the committee justified its proposal by citing the section reading: "All power is inherent in the people, and . . . they have at all times an inalienable and indefeasible right to alter, reform or abolish the government in such a manner as they think proper." Despite minor opposition to emancipation, the meeting passed the committee report. Johnson then appeared on stage to give his hearty approval.[20]

Many prominent unionists quickly endorsed the reconstruction program. In committing themselves to convert the reluctant mass of unionists to unconditional emancipation, they abandoned hope of winning over the secessionists. Consequently, their new crusade coupled persuasion with proscription. Beginning with an election of county officers in March 1864, Johnson required among other things that prospective voters swear active support for federal emancipation measures. His supporters now treated acceptance of emancipation as the test of true loyalty to the Union.[21]

Remembering Lincoln's earlier advocacy of gradual and compensated emancipation, some unionists thought Johnson wanted too much too fast. Daniel C. Trewhitt, an ex-colonel from East Tennessee, and others proposed various alternatives to Johnson's program. Precedents came later in 1864, when West Virginia and Missouri unionists enacted gradual emancipation. Johnson rejected gradualism because it was "like the benefits conferred on the dog in the fable, whose tail was cut off an inch at a time by a humane surgeon, whose kindness of heart would not permit him to remove it at one stroke." His supporters called compensation a financial impossibility for state government. Fortunately for them, Trewhitt switched to Johnson's side and left alternative methods without an effective spokesman. [22]

Antislavery forces nonetheless suffered a major setback in April 1864, when East Tennessee unionist leaders convened. Opponents of the administration attended in large numbers and gained control of the resolutions committee. Its majority reported in favor of strict adherence to the proslavery state constitution; Trewhitt then presented a minority report calling for unconditional emancipation. The ensuing debate revealed a wide range of disagreement. Sam Milligan, Johnson's chief lieutenant, ended the wrangling by moving for adjournment, the only action upon which a majority could agree. To regain some face after this defeat, Johnson engineered a mass meeting at which Knoxville unionists passed antislavery resolutions. Even there, he deemed it necessary to say he hoped unionists would someday receive compensation for slaves. [23]

The conflict over slavery became part of the 1864 presidential contest in Tennessee. Supporters of the administration naturally linked themselves to the Union party, a coalition of Republicans and some War Democrats. Johnson became Lincoln's running mate on a platform calling for immediate emancipation throughout the South. Union Party leaders in Tennessee pragmatically pointed out that wartime stresses had caused slavery to break down in much of the state. They considered legal recognition of the freedom of contrabands to be a prerequisite to the ending of social chaos and a reordering of race relations. Also linking emancipation with nationalism, party leaders contended that slavery caused the Union's breakup by fostering a craving for aristocratic government and a paranoia about the institution's security; slavery then must die so the nation could continue living. [24]

The most inflammatory argument used by Johnson and his

cohorts interwove class antagonism with race prejudice, just as Hinton Rowan Helper, a North Carolinian, had done in his controversial prewar book *The Impending Crisis.* They contended that large planters had used the wealth and power gained from black labor to lord over nonslaveholders economically, socially, and politically. The Chattanooga *Gazette* asked "what poor man's son does not remember his school boy days, when the fact of his father's not owning niggers was continually thrown in his face."[25] Viewing the blacks as insurmountably inferior, most unionists argued that racial equality could not possibly result from emancipation. They felt that the black race would either remain in a subordinate position or become extinct without slavery's paternalistic care. On the other hand, the Reverend Bowen and Samuel C. Mercer, leaders of a small group of emerging radicals, coupled class-conflict arguments with morality instead of prejudice. Appeals to either class antagonism or morality met with resentment from some unionists who accepted emancipation but made it clear that "we pass no judgment upon slaveholders."[26] Diversity of opinion within the Tennessee Union party stood out as its greatest vulnerability.

Dissident unionists formed the Conservative party in affiliation with the Conservative National Union Committee, an organization based in New York City that sought to restructure the Democratic party by ejecting antiwar members and attracting all opponents of emancipation. The committee's scheme failed, but Tennessee Conservatives still endorsed the Democratic presidential ticket because of its hostility to emancipation.[27]

The arguments of Conservatives reflected the Democratic party's Jacksonian ideology. They decried the federal government's interference with local law and self-government under military occupation. Following a strict interpretation of the state constitution, they denounced the proposed convention as unconstitutional and treated emancipation as a violation of the white majority's will. A Conservative newspaper sarcastically added: "It must be quietly borne, if the right of personal liberty, free speech, free press, and a free ballot are all lost to the white man, in a struggle to place Cuffie and Dinah in a position for which they are totally unfit."[28] Conservatives knew that majority opinion as well as existing state law favored slavery's preservation. Only needing to convince unionists to retain the prewar status quo, they faced an easier political task than the Union party.

Conservative party spokesmen flatly denied the evil effects of slavery but charged that emancipation would hurt society. It would perpetuate sectional conflict in a more intense form, and still worse "They may turn loose millions of ignorant negroes to riot over their freedom and to devour the land." Conservatives rejected the Union party's contention that slavery had deteriorated beyond recovery: "The abolitionists in Nashville and elsewhere have continued to repeat that 'slavery is dead' until they have created a doubt of the fact." Conservatives even resurrected the old secessionist claim that Republicans had plotted from the beginning to abolish slavery and to establish racial equality.[29]

Conservative attacks heightened tensions within the Union party. At the latter's state convention in September, three proslavery members of the resolutions committee denounced emancipation, saying it would hurt the party at the polls. That night, they must have come under intense party pressure, for two withdrew their names from the minority report the next morning. The convention then committed the party by adopting resolutions for immediate emancipation.[30] United, the Union party could direct all of its energy against the Conservatives during the final months of the campaign.

The Union party held a major advantage through its connection with the military government. The Johnson regime instigated the arrest of Conservative editor Edwin Paschal when his Nashville *Press* argued that Lincoln's emancipation policy had changed the nature of the war and therefore entitled soldiers to release from military contracts. The arrest intimidated Conservatives and gained the Union party a propaganda victory when a military court convicted Paschal of "Aiding and Encouraging the Rebellion." Johnson also aided his party, as well as his own candidacy, by requiring voters to swear unconditional support for all federal war measures. Conservatives protested that the oath would bar them from voting and withdrew their electoral ticket when Lincoln refused to overrule it.[31] The Union party thus assured itself of a lopsided victory in Tennessee.

The campaign to convert rank-and-file unionists to emancipation began to meet with some success when several local meetings endorsed the idea. After listening to an antislavery speech by Johnson at Knoxville, a soldier remarked that "the citizens concurred most enthusiastically with him." Observers thought the party primarily attracted poor nonslaveholders but that nationalism drew in some slaveholders too. By one unofficial estimate, 11,400 unionists, only 8 percent of the 1860 election turnout, showed at least a tacit acceptance of slavery's end by voting the Union ticket.[32]

During the presidential campaign, just as unionists were being won over to emancipation, Tennessee black leaders became more aggressive. They sought a direct voice in the political process that was reshaping their race's legal status. Black suffrage was not without precedent in the state, for free black men had enjoyed the vote until they were constitutionally disfranchised in 1834. Because politics ranked as one of the most popular pastimes in nineteenth-century America, slaves often knew something about it. Their desire for the ballot in 1864 illustrated their persistent drive for higher status inasmuch as few privileges offered more prestige in American society.[33]

An emerging black political leadership made the demand for

suffrage a major theme at mass meetings and marches.[34] Table 7 shows that most identifiable speakers and organizers were either businessmen or clergymen. Sergeants from black regiments occasionally gave speeches, but military duties appear to have prevented any deeper involvement. Most leaders were free men who had previously achieved social or economic prominence in the black community.[35] Few held a leading position for long. Peter Lowery, Abraham Smith, William Sumner, and Nelson Walker, all from Nashville, stand out as influential and energetic spokesmen for equal rights through the war and Reconstruction.[36]

For advice and encouragement, the leaders looked to their Northern counterparts, who had long agitated for suffrage. The Nashville and Memphis black communities, along with those in six other slave states, sent delegates to the National Convention of Colored Men, held at Syracuse, New York, in October 1864. Ransom Harris, Morris Henderson, Peter Lowery, Horatio N. Rankin, and Abraham Smith did not speak at the convention but participated in the unanimous vote for resolutions demanding emancipation and full citizenship rights. To reach these goals, the convention founded the Equal Rights League. Ransom Harris, a shadowy figure from Nashville, won a seat on the league's national executive board, and Abraham Smith, a contraband who had served as porter for the state legislature, became vice-president for Tennessee. Several months later, a Nashville group established a state chapter of the league under the presidency of Andrew Tate, a free boatman.[37]

During the presidential contest, blacks attended several Union party rallies and on one occasion joined a mob of white Federals in breaking up a Conservative mass meeting. In Nashville, they held a torchlight procession to demonstrate support for the Lincoln-Johnson ticket. Wade Hickman and William Sumner, black businessmen in Nashville, set up a mock polling place for men of their race on election day. The

Table 7. Identifiable Black Political Leaders in Tennessee, 1864–1865

Name	Legal Status	Occupation
	KNOXVILLE	
Alfred E. Anderson	Free	Methodist preacher, teacher
David Scaggs	Free	Tailor
	MEMPHIS	
John Brown	Free	Barber
Warren Brown	?	Sergeant
Joseph Caldwell	Free	Drayman
Morris Henderson	Slave	Baptist minister
Louis Murray	?	Sergeant
David Randolph	?	Baptist preacher
John C. Skurlock	?	Sergeant
Horatio N. Rankin	Free Northerner	Teacher, militia chaplain
W. Woolford	?	African Methodist Episcopal minister
	NASHVILLE	
James Caffrey	Free	Farmer
Anderson Cheatham[a]	Free	Grocer, liquor dealer
Ben J. Hadley	Slave	Liquor dealer
Henry Harding	Slave	Construction contractor, liquor dealer, hotel keeper
Wade Hickman	Slave	Liquor dealer
Daniel Lapsly	?	Barber
Peter Lowery[a]	Free	Disciples of Christ preacher, livery stable operator, general business agent
Samuel Lowery	Free	Disciples of Christ missionary

continued

[a]Known to have been manumitted before the war.

Table 7, continued

Name	Legal Status	Occupation
John McGowen	Free	Barber
H. J. Maxwell	Free Northerner	Sergeant
Alfred Menifee	Free	Grocer
Napoleon Merry	Free	Methodist preacher, stone mason
Nelson Merry[a]	Free	Baptist minister
William C. Napier	Free	Hack driver
Frank Parrish[a]	Free	Barber
Hardy Perry[a]	Free	Hack line operator
George Scott[b]	Free	Shoemaker or pressman
William B. Scott	Free	Editor of Nashville *Colored Tennessean*
Abraham Smith	Slave	Porter at the state capitol building
Jerry Stothart[a]	Free	Hack driver
George Sumner	Free	Hack driver
James Sumner	Free	Hack driver
W. Alex Sumner	Free	Hack driver
William Sumner	Free	Livery stable operator, liquor dealer, grocer
Andrew Tate	Free	Boatman
Daniel Wadkins	Free	Disciples of Christ preacher, teacher, farm laborer
Nelson Walker[a]	Free	Barber

[a]Known to have been manumitted before the war.
[b]The 1860 census lists two free blacks with this name.

3,464 "votes" cast, all but one for the Union party, showed that a significant amount of political interest had evolved.[38]

No whites participated in the activities of the blacks, and few, even among Northern reformers, approved. Colonel Mussey privately favored black suffrage, but a woman who taught blacks in Nashville considered it "quite in advance of the times."[39] Although Bowen and possibly some other radicals favored enfranchisement, they prudently declined to raise the issue during the presidential campaign. Opponents of black suffrage felt no such inhibitions. Gallatin whites showed their disapproval by keeping doors and blinds shut as a march passed. Memphis and Nashville whites hurled rocks and insults at marchers; on two occasions in Nashville, blacks fired shots at the rock-throwers, a response that intensified white criticism.[40] Politicians from both parties openly denounced political equality. Although Johnson appreciated the endorsement of the blacks, he refused to support their enfranchisement in return: "The government of the United States and the governments of the States . . . *are the governments of the free white man,* and to be controlled and administered by him, and the negro must assume that status to which the laws of an enlightened, moral and high-toned society shall assign him."[41]

Despite his stand on political equality, Johnson's racial prejudices were tempered by his vice-presidential campaign and, possibly, by his growing friendship with the abolitionist Mussey. On November 13 Johnson told a black crowd: "I claim . . . every honest man, be he white or colored, as my brother. I am interested in whatever elevates, improves, and ennobles either a people or individual." Wanting to achieve emancipation in Tennessee before he entered national office, he once asked a black audience: "Is there no Moses who will arise and lead these people to freedom?" A listener responded: "You shall be our Moses, Governor?" The egotistical Johnson agreed: "Yes, if no other deliverer will come to you, I will be your Moses, and help to secure and perpetuate your freedom."[42]

Although the "prophet" who made these campaign speeches seems very different from the president who vetoed civil rights legislation, Johnson's behavior patterns show continuity. From early in his political career, he held Jacksonian convictions along with prejudices against blacks, sectionalists, and the wealthy. As military governor during reorganization of the state

113

government, he showed he could stretch Jacksonian beliefs in strict constitutional interpretation and majority rule to great lengths to meet immediate political needs. More importantly, the momentary state of his relations with the objects of his biases could either inflame or moderate those feelings. In 1864 he enjoyed the support of blacks as he battled against Southern sectionalists and aristocrats. The situation and his political alignments would reverse after the war.

Johnson demonstrated some flexibility in setting political priorities, but a rigid commitment followed every controversial decision. Under trying circumstances, he endorsed emancipation during the war and quick restoration of Southern civil government after the war. The first decision showed his dedication to national unity despite the blacks' gain; the second upheld Jacksonian states' rights principles despite the advantage to Southern sectionalists. Determined to retain face after shifting position, he felt personally offended by attacks on his decisions and responded vehemently. Although capable of shrewd political maneuvering, he was too emotional to be a truly Machiavellian figure.[43]

Johnson could not always keep his own supporters under control. A mere four days after the 1864 election, the Union party executive committee for East Tennessee, probably at Brownlow's instigation, called a state convention to nominate a single slate of candidates for constitutional convention delegates. Startled by this precipitate act, Johnson's political associates on the executive committee for Middle Tennessee took sixteen days to consider matters and then issued a call for a convention at the same time and place as the East Tennessee call "to take such steps as wisdom may direct to restore the state of Tennessee to its once honored status in the great National Union."[44] The wording, as later events would show, indicated that Johnson had decided to give the convention a much larger role than the East Tennessee committee had intended.

114

When the meeting convened in Nashville on January 9, 1865, Sam Milligan, probably speaking for Johnson, proposed that the group turn itself into a constitutional convention. Many delegates feared that the public would never accept the legitimacy of this method for accelerating reconstruction, and the convention adopted it only by a small margin after four days of heated debate.[45]

The business committee presented a slate of constitutional amendments that included general emancipation and then suffrage just for black soldiers. The former fulfilled a party commitment made in the presidential campaign and provoked no opposition on the floor. The latter resulted partly from the agitation of blacks and stirred up much controversy. The convention had received a petition circulated by the Tennessee Equal Rights League, which stated: "This is not a Democratic Government if a numerous, law-abiding, industrious, and useful class of citizens, born and bred on the soil, are to be treated . . . as an inferior degraded class, who must have no voice in the Government which they support, protect and defend." Outside pressure from blacks exerted the most influence upon a handful of delegates who privately feared that their party would lose control of the state to ex-Confederates after the war unless freedmen gained the vote. Only Horace Maynard and James R. Hood, editor of the Chattanooga *Gazette*, publicly defended the proposal, arguing that the heroism of black troops in the Battle of Nashville proved their worthiness to vote. Johnson, Brownlow, and many others denounced the proposal as ill timed or too egalitarian. In the end, the convention submitted amendments that did not grant black soldiers suffrage but, through Maynard's efforts, empowered the next general assembly to revise suffrage qualifications.[46]

Because Union party leaders knew that emancipation remained controversial, they feared that a low voter turnout in the referendum would endanger public acceptance of the amendments and of the new state officials to be elected subsequently. In addition, Lincoln would not recognize a reconstructed state government unless the voter turnout was at least 10 percent of the 1860 level. The party's campaign stressed the importance of regaining local self-government and repeated antislavery arguments used in the 1864 election.[47] Most Conservatives, considering the Nashville convention to be unconstitutional and faced with another proscriptive oath for voters, ignored the referendum. Contrabands inevitably displayed strong interest in it and at a Union party rally in Nashville boldly expressed disapproval of a speaker's racist arguments. Voter turnout on referendum day, February 22, exceeded the 1864 total and Lincoln's minimum but still represented only 19 percent of the 1860 amount. White unionists voted 27,684 to 133 to give up slavery, which made Tennessee the sixth Southern state under unionist rule to enact immediate emancipation. In gratitude, the Nashville black community presented Johnson with a $350 gold watch honoring his "Untiring Energy in the Cause of Freedom." Shortly afterward, Brownlow was elected governor, and a Union party slate of legislators won seats without significant opposition.[48] Johnson, who had accomplished his goals, left Tennessee for the vice-presidency.

The state's white electorate always possessed the power, if not the inclination, to abolish slavery. Because most whites accepted the institution before the war, emancipation required a number of them to undergo a major change of attitude. The multidimensional conflicts of the Civil War caused that to happen. Many slaves fled from both unionist and secessionist masters to serve the federal government and to demand a higher status. Unionists bitterly divided over their federal allies' plan to use emancipation as a weapon against the secessionist enemy. Caught between the movements toward emancipation by the federal government and by the contrabands, administration unionists eventually collaborated in order to retain ascendancy over Conservative and secessionist opponents. Therefore, by the time of the referendum, a significant minority of Tennesseans had seen their views of slavery recast in the furnace of war. The fact that they were a minority constituted a bad sign for the future.

8

End of an Institution

On April 5, 1865, the day appointed for inaugurating Tennessee's new civil government, the capitol building was decorated with a gigantic banner that bore antislavery quotations from the Founding Fathers set alongside pictures of black soldiers and schoolchildren. Shortly before William G. Brownlow appeared to take the governor's oath of office, the legislature unanimously ratified the Thirteenth Amendment, which would write slavery's end into the U.S. Constitution.[1] Whether the freedmen's freedom would include more or fewer privileges than the contrabands exercised remained to be seen. But then, freedom had not yet become a reality for all the slaves in the state.

A law's effectiveness depends upon the degree of its acceptance and enforcement. Proslavery convictions ran deep, and many masters ignored the referendum's result. The new state government, which enjoyed scant public respect, few financial resources, and little physical power, could not by itself prevail over the obstinancy of slaveholders. The Union party would continue to rely heavily upon the federal army to enforce unpopular policies.

As the spring of 1865 progressed, major Confederate armies surrendered and the war ended. Within two weeks of Brownlow's inauguration, Lincoln's assassination elevated

Johnson to the presidency. He decided to reconstruct the nation quickly upon the basis of emancipation for slaves and forgiveness for most Confederates. Some rebel veterans came home willing to forget the past; more returned embittered by the destruction of their proslavery nation and blamed defeat not only on the superior power of the Federals, but also on contraband and unionist support of the enemy. The federal government's exaltation of its southern allies pained ex-Confederates all the more. In Maury County, paroled Confederates talked so much about reviving slavery that rural freedmen flooded Columbia, a federal garrison town.[2] Returning soldiers and refugees sharply reduced the proportional weight of blacks in the state population and increased white resistance to social change.

The Conservative party tried to mobilize popular discontent during the congressional election campaign in the summer of 1865. William B. Campbell and Emerson Etheridge openly attacked the constitutionality of the Nashville convention. When Etheridge spoke at Dresden, the audience resolved that the convention was an illegitimate attempt to "subvert and abolish the most important provisions of the Constitution."[3]

Brownlow reacted to the dissension by ordering the arrest of candidates engaged in what he called "nullifying the Constitution." Etheridge landed in a military prison, and Campbell narrowly averted arrest by taking a certified oath of loyalty to the state constitution. President Johnson publicly approved Brownlow's action and ordered the army to continue sustaining the state government. General George H. Thomas, now commanding all troops in the state, kept Etheridge confined until after the election. A sobered Campbell closed his congressional campaign by declaring: "I now regard slavery as abolished, and expect the [Thirteenth] constitutional amendment to be adopted . . . I do not desire to resurrect it, nor do the people of Tennessee."[4] Confronted by federal military might, political resistance to emancipation collapsed.

119

Recalcitrant slaveholders continued to defy the authorities and retain blacks under unchanged conditions. A few kept them isolated and unaware of emancipation through most or all of 1865; others, suspecting their wards had heard about the referendum, denounced it as false and sometimes used force.[5] After shooting a disobedient slave on July 2, Amos Black warned his other bondsmen: "You have been fooled with the d——d Yankee lies till you thought you were free, and you got so you could not obey your master. There is no law against killing niggers & I will kill every d——d one I have, if they do not obey me and work just as they did before the war." Vigilante bands and guerrillas maintained slavery in Hickman, Dyer, Gibson, Carroll, Weakley, and Haywood counties at least through early summer. In some parts of the state, the institution remained fully alive as late as September 1865.[6]

The federal army and the Freedmen's Bureau, a new War Department agency responsible for supervising the transition from slavery to freedom, held public meetings around the state and convinced some masters to acknowledge the freedom of blacks.[7] However, where masters forcibly preserved slavery, armed intervention became necessary. Federal patrols could curtail vigilante and guerrilla activity, but violence committed by individuals was more difficult to control. The Freedmen's Bureau punished the perpetrators, if a black could escape and report the cruel treatment.[8] Enslaved children particularly needed help. One little girl, kept locked in her master's house ever since her relatives ran away, was finally released by her brother and an armed Federal after the state referendum. The Freedmen's Bureau, the army, and the courts all issued orders returning children to parents.[9] The termination of slavery required determined action by civil and military powers.

John S. Claybrooke, who had large slaveholdings in Haywood and Williamson counties, observed that, wherever the army went to announce emancipation, slaves "become by degrees of no use to us." After Federals informed one Haywood County slave of her freedom, she slacked off in the performance of her uncompensated work. When the mistress threatened to whip her, she retorted that the mistress no longer had any such right; the slave's shocked and disbelieving husband silenced her with a blow. Several days later, because of the wife's prodding, the couple visited the county courthouse to inquire about their legal status. Upon confirming that their mistress had withheld the news of emancipation, they left to seek employment elsewhere.[10]

News of emancipation transformed many loyal slaves, who were thrilled by the prospect of new opportunities and privileges. For those who had remained with owners because that had seemed the most advantageous choice, compensated employment usually seemed even better. Blacks who had seen slavery as their inevitable lot quickly comprehended that their status was changing. One mistress discovered that her previously loyal charges deliberately left her for paying jobs on the day of the referendum. Even slaves who were very affectionate toward their masters sometimes acquired new aspirations and tried to part on friendly terms.[11]

The institution did not end on a pleasant note for all loyal slaves. One in Davidson County who had resisted peer pressure to run away during the war was startled by her master's fury over emancipation: "He was gonna kill me 'cause I was free. I got shame about it, they talked about it so." She grew disillusioned about her friendly attitude toward the owner's family and eventually left to work for someone else. Loyal slaves who learned about their freedom from outside sources often assumed trusted masters would compensate them fairly after the fall harvest, but masters who did not announce emancipation usually did not intend to pay wages. The disappointed freedmen felt betrayed. If they became contentious, the ex-owners usually drove them off the premises.[12] Emancipation revealed to loyal slaves just how much reality lay behind the benevolent image of the masters.

Independence shocked those loyal slaves who were thoroughly accustomed to routine or possibly lulled by paternalism. Some continued to serve the ex-owner, though they received only subsistence in return. William Coleman, from Jackson, feared working for a stranger and knew of no white who might hire him. Because his old master wanted to run the freedmen off the farm, Coleman was forced to beg permission to keep working for just room and board. Anna Lee, of Huntsville, needed time to observe and adjust to the new order: "Thank God our Maser was able to keep us and see after us until we had kind of got use to being free and to where we was not afraid to ask a man for a job."[13]

A few slaves were so attached to paternalistic owners that they ignored their freedom for a time. When one Williamson County planter concluded his announcement of emancipation with tearful pleas for the freedmen to stay, they all agreed to work without wages through the rest of the year. Henry, a faithful servant to a Confederate veteran, tired of black Federals calling him one of the "Secesh Niggers who didn't have no better sense than to be slaves to a Secesh master!" He eventually found another job and moved to a lot his ex-owner gave him in a black neighborhood. Some freedmen remained with their old masters for life, which earned fond remembrances in autobiographies.[14]

Masters naturally resented the institution's end. Mass meetings at Memphis and La Grange in May 1865 refused to consider resolutions approving emancipation. C. R. Hall, an East Tennessee unionist, complained for years afterward about the federal government's failure to compensate unionist slaveholders. Robert H. Cartmell, of Madison County, accepted slavery's passing with grim stoicism: "Without approving I must abide by and support the fact or law or proclamation, just as I support *all laws*, whether constitutional or no. They must be obeyed until declared null & void. This *one* never will."[15]

In late 1865 hope for the institution's preservation or restoration rapidly disappeared. The state supreme court had ruled favorably on the emancipation amendment's constitutionality. A federal military court found Etheridge guilty of denying the amendment's legitimacy but released him without punishment. Given the firmness of President Johnson's commitment to emancipation, Conservatives and former secessionists turned to loud acceptances of slavery's end in the hope that this concession would prevent further advances in the status of blacks. Little choice remained anyway, for on December 18, 1865, completion of the Thirteenth Amendment's ratification permanently settled the matter.[16]

Emancipation produced more questions than answers. The story of how the difficult issues of economic and social readjustment were resolved belongs more properly in a history of Tennessee's postwar reconstruction; the final portion of this study will only present a brief overview of the immediate implications of emancipation. Abolition unquestionably meant that freedmen were no longer property, and that inherently gave them some sort of higher status. Specific possibilities ranged from supervised serfdom to full equality. Contrabands had pioneered their own alternatives to slavery during the war, but without continued outside intervention the odds stood against significant change, for social systems tend to preserve or parallel old traits in adjusting to a new order.[17]

Slavery's end exerted a major impact on the economy. For one thing, it caused a substantial loss of invested capital. The assessed value of Tennessee's taxable slaves in 1860 had exceeded $114 million. The only compensation program resulted from the Federal government's promise of $300 for each slave whom a unionist enlisted. A claims commission sat for three months in 1867 and paid just sixty claims to Tennesseans before

Congress terminated it. Fiscal losses from emancipation combined with those from Confederate bonds, Confederate currencies, and property destruction to set back the entire state economy.[18]

Depressed economic conditions made the payment of people who had once worked merely for subsistence even more distasteful and difficult. Some whites treated freedmen employees in a fair and friendly way; others physically abused and shortchanged them on payday. The exploiters either cloaked their actions in paternalistic rhetoric or blatantly held that a black "will only labor under the incentives of pain and penalties. Persuasions will not move him, nor has wealth any allurement."[19] Most planters wanted to restrict freedmen to the position of landless, low-income laborers.

Freedmen, like contrabands, aspired to a better income, economic independence, or both. Differing aims caused much contention between the races during the transition in the labor system. Freedmen used their freedom to choose employers as an economic weapon. Migrating and delaying the signing of contracts helped to arrange better deals; taking only irregular work helped to maintain independence. The resulting uncertainties and rural labor shortage disrupted the economy. Furthermore, aggrieved freedmen could be more disobedient and disrespectful laborers than slaves had been. They readily took complaints to the Freedmen's Bureau for adjudication; much quitting and firing took place in 1865 as well. White attempts to preserve slavery and black rejection of it made both sides distrustful of the other.[20]

Freedmen occupied a weak position in the postwar economy. Emancipation in 1865, like wartime flight, usually left blacks with no resources except their ability to work, and the war's end narrowed the options for earning a living. The federal army's demobilization drastically reduced opportunities for government jobs. The Freedmen's Bureau, hoping to hasten economic recovery, forced hundreds of irregularly employed blacks to leave towns for farm work.[21] Restoration of civil government emboldened several local courts to revive enforcement of the law prohibiting black businesses.[22] Returning war refugees reclaimed their farms from ex-slaves who had used the land for personal profit. In at least a few counties, whites used social pressure or vigilante violence to prevent freedmen from becoming tenant farmers.[23] It is no wonder that most former slaves continued to fill the plantation system's need for a large supply of cheap, unskilled laborers.

Labor contracts needed to be approved by the Freedmen's Bureau, which did not set minimum wages or behavioral rules as Adjutant General Thomas had done in his wartime contract labor system. Perpetuating one paternalistic aspect of slavery, compensation under postwar contracts usually included some or all subsistence needs. Although the whole income of hands who worked for shares cannot be determined, the data in table 8 shows that wage laborers who signed contracts at the bureau in 1865 earned less than contrabands did under the contract labor system in 1864. Wages would fall further during postwar deflation.[24] Compensated labor represented an advancement over slavery, yet offered scant opportunity for economic mobility.

Like other nineteenth-century Americans, freedmen regarded the acquisition of a small farm as the key to economic security. A black Baptist preacher wrote: "We think the government ought in justice to the race provide for them obtaining farms at such prices and on such terms as would enable our people in a reasonable time to have a home of their own on which they might hope to earn a living & educate their children." Congress had encouraged such hopes by empowering the Freedmen's Bureau to rent forty-acre plots of confiscatable abandoned land, to which lessees would have a preemptory right for purchasing a possessory title later. News of the law spread among freedmen and prompted one group in Robertson County to take over their former master's plantation for a time. However, contrary to folklore, not all freedmen believed that land redistribution would occur.[25]

Table 8. Average Monthly Wages
of Adult Freedmen
Hired in Tennessee during 1865

Other Elements of Compensation	Males	Females
	(numbers in parentheses)	
Room, board, clothes, and medical care	$ 4.80 (19)	$4.46 (13)
Room, board, and clothes	9.34 (18)	4.04 (20)
Room, board, and medical care	12.09*(145)	8.08*(83)
Room and board	10.54 (120)	6.72 (93)

*These figures should not be greater than those in the next line; probably the limited number of surviving contracts skewed the results.

Bureau officials in Tennessee prepared preliminary plans for land redistribution, but President Johnson canceled the program because it conflicted with his lenient Reconstruction policy toward former secessionists. Had the bureau carried out the program, lessees would have encountered vigilante violence, just as the tenant farmers did in 1865. The example of British Jamaica had shown planters that, if freedmen withdrew from the labor market to become self-sufficient farmers, the plantation system would suffer. Even if federal forces could have succeeded in suppressing inevitable white resistance, blacks would still face financial dangers in an era when rising operational cost would eliminate many small farms. Worst of all, the courts might interpret the Constitution's treason clause as terminating possessory titles and reverting the land to heirs when the previous owner died.[26] By itself, the land provision in the

Freedmen's Bureau Act provided no panacea for troubled race relations.

After abandoning plans for land redistribution, the Freedmen's Bureau turned increasingly toward a laissez-faire policy. Late in the war, various politicians charged that paternalistic programs were repressing blacks, creating excessive expense, or overexpanding governmental powers. As a result, Congress wrote the Freedmen's Bureau Act in laissez-faire terms.[27]

When the bureau took over operation of the Freedmen's Departments in the South, a turnover of personnel followed, which facilitated a policy change. Brigadier General Clinton B. Fisk, the new bureau head in Tennessee, held that "there is no preventive for suffering among the freedmen save such as they themselves furnish or succor except in industry. Let them *work.*" During the fall, when the bureau mercilessly closed contraband camps and hospitals, it issued departing freedmen only small amounts of food and clothing. "Just about relief enough," one teacher observed, "to prevent the executive officers of the government from hearing the cry of distress."[28] One freedmen's aid society purchased the Nashville contraband camp to establish a home for the neediest blacks, who were the orphaned, elderly, sick, and handicapped. Northern charitable contributions as a whole declined after the war, and new benevolent societies that freedmen founded in Nashville, Murfreesboro, and Chattanooga could not make up the difference.[29]

Emancipation had explicit implications for the social status of freedmen. They fell under the state code for free blacks, which, as chapter 3 showed, had mostly fallen into disuse during the war. No consensus could be reached on what should be done about it. Some whites now demanded the enactment of a more restrictive code, and radical members of the Union party called for a repeal of the old black laws. A legislative deadlock resulted and prevented significant revision of the laws during 1865.[30]

Meanwhile, several towns and counties had resumed enforcement of laws forbidding blacks from selling merchandise and
whites from selling liquor to them. Knoxville prohibited them
from possessing firearms, and Tullahoma established a curfew
for them.[31] Freedmen quickly learned that the inadmissibility
of their testimony against whites in court could place them in
serious jeopardy. White policemen, judges, and juries showed
little leniency, if not some prejudice, toward freedmen. By the
end of 1865 the black proportion of the state penitentiary population had risen from a prewar 2 percent to 33 percent.[32] Court
fines and incarceration had replaced the slaveholder's whip as
the legal means of physically controlling blacks.

Concern that curtailment of the newly won freedom of blacks
would tarnish the federal victory prompted interference with
the restored Southern civil governments. General George H.
Thomas, whose racial attitudes had changed during the Battle
of Nashville, declared martial law in Columbia when the town
jailed two black schoolgirls under excessive bail for a minor
incident of trespassing and rock-throwing. The Freedmen's Bureau in Tennessee, as in other Southern states, assumed judicial jurisdiction over cases involving blacks on the grounds that
the state violated freedmen's rights by restricting their testimony. By establishing its own courts, the bureau ended most
black code prosecutions; by promising to close its courts as
soon as the legislature granted equal judicial rights to blacks, it
pushed the state toward civil rights legislation. Federal and
black pressure brought about the desired changes during 1866
and 1867.[33]

Emancipation affected social relations between the races by
eliminating the slave class and raising those people to the position of free blacks. Because free blacks had been a small, exceptional group, the sudden expansion of the class would likely
lead to its redefinition. The results of wartime efforts by contrabands and reformers set much of the new pattern. Essen-

tially, freedmen sought to enjoy the same social rights as whites while minimizing institutional connections between the races.

Independent black congregations continued to sprout from the underground slave religion. White trustees of black chapels either gracefully granted the parishioners independence or spitefully evicted them from the buildings. Now that religious freedom had been won, blacks began constructing new denominational structures.[34]

Freedmen also liberated their family life from white control and reunited relatives who had belonged to different owners. Those who had several mates under different masters were forced to make a difficult choice, and even then the desired spouse might choose otherwise. Children who had lived with only one parent went through a difficult period of adjustment when a second adult moved in. The Freedmen's Bureau, like the wartime Freedmen's Departments, wanted to sanctify the family through legal safeguards. If a county government refused to issue marriage licenses to blacks or to handle their adultery and bastardy cases, the Bureau did so.[35]

Although literate freedmen and Northern reformers opened numerous new schools for blacks throughout the state, by September 1865 they had enrolled only about 9,000 students, a small proportion of the uneducated. To increase educational opportunities and decrease the high student-teacher ratio (66:1), the Freedmen's Bureau established a teacher-training program for blacks at Nashville in January 1866 (it would evolve into Fisk University). The bureau also lobbied for the creation of a state public school system, which the legislature instituted in 1867.[36]

Because of either paternalistic influence or their own brand of pragmatism, some freedmen continued to behave as submissively and deferentially as slaves had toward whites, but hopes engendered by emancipation made increasing numbers more self-assertive. Black soldiers, who were mustered out in late 1865 and early 1866, pushed other freedmen to abandon demeaning rituals of racial etiquette. A few of them attempted without success to defy customary segregation in public places.[37] Black communities in small towns held meetings to demand equal rights and to organize their own institutions. In August 1865 the first in a series of state black conventions met in Nashville to lobby for the franchise, which was not won until 1867.[38] As it had during the war, black assertiveness would play a key role during Reconstruction.

The stereotype of free blacks as lazy, criminal, and seditious remained widespread; their new assertiveness inflamed old prejudices. Influenced by divergent lines of proslavery thought, whites commonly advocated either close paternalistic supervision or naked force to control and subordinate freedmen.[39] Whereas the first group approved of black education and biracial churches, provided white Southerners did the teaching and preaching, the second group tried to halt both through social pressure and violence.[40] Some paternalists called for a colonization program to allow blacks a separate self-development; some unabashed racists advocated it to eliminate the race from American society. Most white Tennesseans demanded that they—not the federal government, Northern reformers, or freedmen—should determine the new status of blacks.[41] Racial prejudice and the caste mentality had survived the destruction of slavery to fester and break out in new forms.

Opponents of black advancement may have conceded slavery's demise, but they were not ready to end social subordination and economic exploitation. White resistants from the ranks of both ex-Confederates and unionists turned increasingly to extralegal violence, the traditional method of emergency racial control that gained in effectiveness as the federal army demobilized.[42] Although reactionary forces eventually overthrew the Union party's rule in Tennessee, they could not eliminate the most rudimentary of the economic, legal, and social privileges that blacks had won.

Tennesseans both prevented and accomplished changes in race relations through struggle. Neither Reconstruction nor slavery died easily, and both left vestiges behind. Freedmen gained a larger zone of privacy because emancipation weakened several institutional controls that whites had exercised over them. Poverty, the numerical superiority of whites, caste barriers, and racial prejudices continued to set outer bounds upon black lives. When interviewed during the Great Depression, a few Tennessee ex-slaves understandably longed for the guaranteed subsistence of slavery, yet most agreed with the freedman who asserted that "they have more privileges now, in some things anyhow. I rather be out of slavery than in, all the time."[43]

Notes

AFIC   American Freedmen's Inquiry Commission Testimony (all citations under this abbreviation are to file VII, which was taken on November 23, 1863), Record Group 94, National Archives

AMA   American Missionary Association Archives (all citations are to the Tennessee file), Amistad Research Center, Dillard University, New Orleans

AS   George P. Rawick, ed., *The American Slave: A Composite Autobiograhy* (41 vols., Westport, Conn., 1972–79)

ER–1863   John Eaton to John A. Rawlins, April 29, 1863 (a general report), American Freedmen's Inquiry Commission Testimony, file VI, Record Group 94, National Archives

ER–1864   John Eaton, *Report of the General Superintendent of Freedmen, Department of the Tennessee and State of Arkansas for 1864* (Memphis, 1865)

G.O.   General Order

GPB   Generals' Papers and Books, Record Group 94, National Archives

LR   Letters Received

OR   U.S. War Department, *The War of the Rebellion: A Compilation of the Official Records of the Union and Confederate Armies* (131 vols., Washington, 1880–1901)

NA   National Archives

RG	National Archives Record Group
	RG 24: Records of the Bureau of Naval Personnel
	RG 29: Records of the Bureau of the Census
	RG 94: Records of the Office of the Adjutant General
	RG 105: Records of the Bureau of Refugees, Freedmen, and Abandoned Lands
	RG 108: Records of the Headquarters of the United States Army
	RG 109: Confederate Records
	RG 153: Records of the Office of Judge Advocate General (Army)
	RG 393: Records of the United States Army Continental Commands, 1821–1920
SHC	Southern Historical Collection, University of North Carolina, Chapel Hill, North Carolina
S.O.	Special Order
TSLA	Tennessee State Library and Archives, Nashville, Tennessee
USCA	United States Colored Artillery
USCI	United States Colored Infantry

Introduction

1. Major works dealing with this theme are W. E. Burghardt Du Bois, *Black Reconstruction, 1860–1880* (New York, 1935); Bell Irvin Wiley, *Southern Negroes, 1861–1865* (New Haven, 1938); Benjamin Quarles, *The Negro in the Civil War* (Boston, 1953); Edward Magdol, *A Right to the Land: Essays on the Freedmen's Community* (Westport, Conn., 1977); and Leon F. Litwack, *Been in the Storm So Long: The Aftermath of Slavery* (New York, 1979). Regarding the monument, see William G. Eliot, *The Story of Archer Alexander* (Boston, 1885), 12–14.

2. Eugene D. Genovese, *Roll, Jordan, Roll: The World the Slaves Made* (New York, 1974), 148–49.

3. Paul D. Escott, *Slavery Remembered: A Record of Twentieth-Century Slave Narratives* (Chapel Hill, N.C., 1979), 20, 120;

Magdol, *Right to the Land,* 4–10. Litwack, *Been in the Storm,* 162, 215–16, holds that each interpretation fits a portion of the slave community.

4. Clarence L. Mohr, "Georgia Blacks during Secession and Civil War, 1859–1865" (Ph.D. dissertation, University of Georgia, 1975); Joel Williamson, *After Slavery: The Negro in South Carolina during Reconstruction, 1861–1877* (Chapel Hill, 1965); C. Peter Ripley, *Slaves and Freedmen in Civil War Louisiana* (Baton Rouge, La., 1976); Victor B. Howard, *Black Liberation in Kentucky: Emancipation and Freedom, 1862–1884* (Lexington, Ky., 1983).

Chapter 1

1. Memphis *Appeal,* May 31, June 1, 1861; J. R. and Margrette Paisley to Joseph McLean, May 7, 1861, in Works Progress Administration, "[Tennessee] Civil War Records," 4 vols. of typescript at TSLA, IV, addendum page.

2. C. R. Barteau, *A Brief Review* (Hartsville, Tenn., 1861), passim; Robert H. Cartmell Diary, May 7, 1861, TSLA; John Houston Bills Diary, April 16, 1861, SHC; Albert W. Schroeder, Jr., "Writings of a Tennessee Unionist," *Tennessee Historical Quarterly,* IX (September 1950), 253, 263.

3. Chase C. Mooney, *Slavery in Tennessee* (Bloomington, Ind., 1957), 105, 145; U.S. Department of the Interior, Census Office, *Eighth Census of the United States, 1860: Population* (Washington, 1864), 238–39, 466–67; Tennessee, *Reports from Public Officers and Institutions, 1859–1860* (Nashville, 1860), 18–23.

4. Mooney, *Slavery in Tennessee,* chap. 6.

5. U.S. Census Office, *Eighth Census: Population,* 466–67; U.S. Department of the Interior, Census Office, *Eighth Census of the United States, 1860: Mortality and Miscellaneous Statistics* (Washington, 1866), 337–38; Clarksville *Chronicle,* February 1, 1861.

6. Tennessee, *Code* (Nashville, 1858), secs. 2437, 2605–89, 2808; Mooney, *Slavery in Tennessee,* 13–14; James Merton England, "The Free Negro in Antebellum Tennessee" (Ph.D. dissertation, Vanderbilt University, 1941), 200; Loren Schweninger, "The Free Slave

Phenomenon: James P. Thomas and the Black Community in Ante-Bellum Nashville," *Civil War History*, XXII (December 1976), 302–06; Charles B. Dew, "Black Ironworkers and the Slave Insurrection Panic of 1856," *Journal of Southern History*, XLI (August 1975), 333–38.

7. Marriage Certificates for Shelby, Dyer, and Gibson counties, Commissioner's Records, RG 105, NA. John W. Blassingame, *The Slave Community: Plantation Life in the Antebellum South* (2d ed., New York, 1979), 361, obtains slightly different results by including Wilson County certificates, which are excluded here because their different format does not yield comparable data.

8. *AS*, XVIII, 45, 105, 129, 175 (for just a few of many such references in *AS*); ER-1863, 3. These data contradict the higher estimates in Du Bois, *Black Reconstruction*, 638; Mooney, *Slavery in Tennessee*, 95–96; and Genovese, *Roll, Jordan, Roll*, 563.

9. *AS*, XV, 106, 131, 216; Herman A. Norton, *Tennessee Christians: A History of the Christian Church (Disciples of Christ) in Tennessee* (Nashville, 1971), 128–29; T. C. Fuller, *History of Negro Baptists in Tennessee* (Memphis, 1936), 47; Ira Berlin, *Slaves without Masters: The Free Negro in the Antebellum South* (New York, 1974), 296; *Freedmen's Bulletin*, I (January 1865), 61 (quoted). Many white writers in the nineteenth century tried to phrase black statements in dialect. Because the intent was not always derogatory, this study will use such quotes when they accurately convey important black viewpoints.

10. Thomas L. Webber, *Deep Like the Rivers: Education in the Slave Quarter Community, 1831–1865* (New York, 1978), chaps. 5–6; Albert J. Rabateau, *Slave Religion: The Invisible Institution in the Antebellum South* (New York, 1978), 214–17, 318; *AS*, XVIII, 4, 35, 76, 121 (for just a few of many such references in *AS*). These data do not support the contention in Genovese, *Roll, Jordan, Roll*, 236, that many masters permitted slaves to hold their own Sunday services.

11. Blassingame, *Slave Community*, 172, 311–12.

12. Knoxville *Whig*, May 18, June 8, 1861; Nashville *Union and American*, June 25, 1861; Nashville *Republican Banner*, December 8, 1860; LeRoy P. Graf and Ralph W. Haskins, eds., *The Papers of Andrew Johnson* (6 vols. to date, Knoxville, 1967–), IV, 160–62;

Henry Cooper to M. D. Cooper, April 27, 1861, Cooper Family Papers, TSLA; James Welch Patton, *Unionism and Reconstruction in Tennessee, 1860–1869* (Chapel Hill, 1934), 63, 68.

13. Nashville *Gazette,* May 7, September 28, 1861; Fayetteville *Observer,* March 7, 1861; Nashville *Republican Banner,* March 26, 1861; Wiley, *Southern Negroes,* 11; Tennessee, *Acts,* 33 General Assembly, 2 Extra Sess., 25 (quoted); George Washington Matthews Diary, May 28, 1861, January 18–19, 1862, TSLA. Also see Bills Diary, May 27, 1861.

14. Fayetteville *Observer,* May 2, 9, 1861; Lewisburg *Southern Messenger,* May 1, 1861; Myra Inman Diary, May 13, 1861, SHC; Catherine Watterson to W. H. Watterson, May 20, 1861, Watterson Family Papers, McClung Collection Library, Knoxville; Lizinka Brown to David Hubbard, [May 1861], David Hubbard Papers, TSLA; Cartmell Diary, May 27, 1861. On slave rebellion scares elsewhere, see Steven A. Channing, *Crisis of Fear: Secession in South Carolina* (New York, 1970), 265–74.

15. Bills Nos. 52, 215, 260, House Manuscript Bills, 34 General Assembly, TSLA; Tennessee, *House Journal,* 34 General Assembly, 1 Sess., 199–200 (November 7, 1861).

16. Quarles, *Negro in the Civil War,* 49; Bills Diary, May 22, 1861; H. S. Bradford to Isham Harris, July 17, 1861, Isham Harris Gubernatorial Papers, TSLA; Memphis *Avalanche,* April 29, 1861.

17. Only nine officers' servants appeared in the fugitive slave advertisements in the Chattanooga *Rebel* and Knoxville *Register* between September 1862 and June 1863. Also see George L. Knox, *Slave and Freeman,* ed. by Willard B. Gatewood, Jr. (Lexington, Ky., 1979), 50; and Genovese, *Roll, Jordan, Roll,* 352–53.

18. Files of Silas Gober, Dawson Pugh, Wade Watkins, Sam Collier, Presley Smith, and Ned Gregory, Colored Men's Confederate Pension Applications, TSLA; Coleman Davis Smith file, Confederate Civil War Veterans Questionnaires, TSLA; Orland Kay Armstrong, *Old Massa's People: The Old Slaves Tell Their Story* (Indianapolis, 1931), 197.

19. Quarles, *Negro in the Civil War,* 48; Memphis *Appeal,* November 10, 1861; Gideon J. Pillow, S.O. 140, May 26, 1861, G. J. Pillow Correspondence, RG 109, NA; *OR,* ser. 1, III, 720–21; Bills Diary, October 9, 1861.

20. James A. Rogers to Leonidas Polk, October 23, 1861, A. M. Rafter to James A. Rogers, December 17, 1861, February 10, 1862, James A. Rogers to James A. Mayfield, January 9, 1862 (quoted), and Thomas J. Blackmans to James A. Rogers, [1862], James A. Rogers Papers, Office of the Field Archaeologist for West Tennessee, Pinson, Tenn.

21. Clarksville *Chronicle*, January 10, 1862; *OR*, ser. 1, VII, 711; Kinson McVay to ?, Andrew Johnson Papers, Library of Congress; Henry Yarbrough to Chris C. Cocke, December 27, 1861, in Works Progress Administration, "[Tennessee] Civil War Records," III, 206.

22. *OR*, ser. 4, II, 421; Rolls 5493, 5502, 5506, 5548, Slave Payrolls, RG 109, NA; Nashville *Union*, March 3, 1864; Fayetteville *Observer*, November 20, 1862; Tennessee, *House Journal*, 34 General Assembly, 1 Sess., 431 (March 11, 1862); Wiley, *Southern Negroes*, 89, 117. Real values of the hires were estimated in the same manner as in table 2.

23. Nimrod Porter Diary, January 1, August 4, 1863, SHC; Memphis *Avalanche*, May 1, 1862 (quoted); Rolls 5516, 5535–37, Slave Payrolls, RG 109, NA; Bills Diary, February 3, 1865.

24. *OR*, ser. 1, XXIII, pt. 2, 850, 853, ser. 2, V, 844, 959.

25. Knoxville *Register*, April 1862–July 1863; Chattanooga *Rebel*, September 1862–July 1863.

26. Mohr, "Georgia Blacks," 154–91, finds a contrary pattern in Georgia towns.

27. Table 2 is not a scientific sample, a near-impossibility in this situation. The data came from bills of sale recorded in the deed books of one-third of the state's wartime counties: Bedford, Bradley, Carroll, Coffee, Davidson, Dyer, Giles, Greene, Hawkins, Henry, Hickman, Jefferson, Knox, Lincoln, McMinn, Madison, Marshall, Maury, Monroe, Montgomery, Roane, Rutherford, Smith, Sullivan, Wayne, Williamson, and Wilson. Only bona fide sales of individuals in the peak price range between twelve and forty years of age were considered. Robert W. Fogel and Stanley L. Engerman, *Time on the Cross* (2 vols., Boston, 1974), I, 76, 86–89; Wiley, *Southern Negroes*, 87–90. Reports in the Fayetteville *Observer*, January 23, 1862, Athens *Post*, March 7, 1862, and Greeneville *Banner*, October 24, 1862, confirm the rise in prices.

28. New York *Times*, March 31, October 8, 1865; *Senate Docu-*

ments, 58 Cong., 2 Sess., No. 234, IV, 528, 671, VII, 248, 610–13; *OR*, ser. 1, LII, pt. 2, 592; William H. Harder Memoir, 173–74, TSLA.

Chapter 2

1. May Winston Caldwell, *A Chapter from the Life of a Little Girl of the Confederacy* (Nashville, n.d.), 10. Case studies that describe developments similar to those in this chapter are: Mohr, "Georgia Blacks," chap. 3; Ripley, *Slaves and Freedmen*, chap. 1; Armstead Louis Robinson, "Day of Jubilo: Civil War and the Demise of Slavery in the Mississippi Valley, 1861–1865" (Ph.D. dissertation, University of Rochester, 1976), chaps. 4–5; Willie Lee Rose, *Rehearsal for Reconstruction: The Port Royal Experiment* (Indianapolis, 1964), chap. 4; Tracy Whittaker Schneider, "The Institution of Slavery in North Carolina, 1860–65" (Ph.D. dissertation, Duke University, 1979), chap. 5; Williamson, *After Slavery*, chap. 1; and William L. Woods, "The Travail of Freedom: Mississippi Blacks, 1862–70" (Ph.D. dissertation, Princeton University, 1979), chap. 1. Also see Benjamin Quarles, *The Negro in the American Revolution* (Chapel Hill, N.C., 1961), chaps. 7–8; and Arthur F. Corwin, *Spain and the Abolition of Slavery in Cuba, 1817–1886* (Austin, Tex., 1967), 278–96.

2. Genovese, *Roll, Jordan, Roll*, 133–37, 148–54.

3. Escott, *Slavery Remembered*, 19–20, 120–23; Magdol, *Right to the Land*, 4–10; Wiley, *Southern Negroes*, 19–23, 83–84. Litwack, *Been in the Storm*, 162–63, 182, 300, synthesizes the two positions.

4. Elizabeth Harding to W. G. Harding, April 27, June 29, 1862, Harding-Jackson Papers, SHC; Randall M. Miller, ed., "Letters from Nashville, 1862, II: 'Dear Master,'" *Tennessee Historical Quarterly*, XXXIII (Spring 1974), 87–90 (quoted); 1860 Census, Slaveholder Schedule for Davidson County, RG 29, NA; Cincinnati *Gazette*, August 3, 1865. Also see L. Virginia French Diary, August 10, 17, 1862, TSLA; and Cincinnati *Journal* excerpt in Philadelphia *Press*, August 7, 1863.

5. *AS*, XVIII, 74–75 (quoted), 250, supp. ser. 1, V, 306–08, supp. ser. 2, IX, 3468; Nashville *Tennessean*, August 16, 1936 (supplement); Knox, *Slave and Freeman*, 48; Isaac Lane Interview, Sep-

tember 5, 1932 (quoted), Bell I. Wiley Papers, Emory University Library, Atlanta.

6. *AS*, VII, 74, IX, pt. 4, 196, 273, XIX, 115; Sarah Ridley Trimble, ed., "Behind the Lines in Middle Tennessee, 1863–1865: The Journal of Bettie Ridley Blackmore," *Tennessee Historical Quarterly,* XII (March 1953), 52; Enoch L. Mitchell, ed., "Letters of a Confederate Surgeon in the Army of Tennessee to His Wife," *Tennessee Historical Quarterly,* V (March 1946), 80; Porter Diary, March 25, November 12, 1864; French Diary, August 17 (quoted), 31, 1862, April 26, 1863; Bills Diary, October 2, 1862.

7. Rabateau, *Slave Religion,* 312–13, 318–19; *AS*, XVIII, 259, supp. ser. 1, V, 142–43; T. J. Wright, *History of the Eighth Regiment Kentucky Volunteer Infantry* (St. Joseph, Mo., 1880), 42 (quoted); T. F. Dornblaser, *Sabre Strokes of the Pennsylvania Dragoons in the War of 1861–65* (Philadelphia, 1884), 53 (quoted).

8. Genovese, *Roll, Jordan, Roll,* 272–73, 279; Magdol, *Right to the Land,* 9–15.

9. *AS*, XVIII, 219, XIX, 109–15; Rabateau, *Slave Religion,* 218–19; Knox, *Slave and Freeman,* 46–48; Philadelphia *Press,* November 3, 1862 (quoted).

10. *AS*, XVI, Tenn. sec., 68, XVIII, 4, 113; Wiley, *Southern Negroes,* 16; Louis Hughes, *Thirty Years A Slave: From Bondage to Freedom* (Milwaukee, 1897), 114, 193; Tennessee Civil War Centennial Commission, *Tennesseans in the Civil War* (2 vols., Nashville, 1964), I, 1; U.S. Census Office, *Eighth Census: Population,* 592–93.

11. Bills Diary, July 30, 1862; Joseph E. Washington to Jane Washington, February 9, 1865, Washington Family Papers, TSLA; Sarah Kennedy to David Kennedy, August 19, 1863, Sarah Bailey Kennedy Papers, TSLA; Trimble, ed., "Behind the Lines," 62–63; John N. Barker Diary, January 27, August 21–22, 1864, Clarksville Public Library, Clarksville, Tenn.; Cartmell Diary, November 13, 1862.

12. Trimble, ed., "Behind the Lines," 63 (quoted), 79; Cartmell Diary, March 28, 1863; Mary Reynolds to Simeon Reynolds, May 1, 1864, Mary Reynolds Papers, University of Tennessee Library, Knoxville.

13. Theodore Upson, *With Sherman to the Sea,* ed. by Oscar O. Winter (Baton Rouge, La., 1943), 73 (quoted); Elvira J. Powers, *Hos-*

pital Pencilings (Boston, 1866), 116–18; Edward C. Downs, *The Great American Scout and Spy, "General Bunker"* (3d ed., New York, 1870), 79–82, 109–11, 126; George H. Thomas Journal, May 1, August 31, 1863, GPB; John Y. Simon, ed., *The Papers of Ulysses S. Grant* (10 vols. to date, Carbondale, Ill., 1967–), V, 86; *OR*, ser. 1, XVII, pt. 2, 238.

14. Simon, ed., *Grant Papers*, V, 87; *OR*, ser. 1, XVI, pt. 2, 269, ser. 2, IV, 291; Cartmell Diary, February 21, 1865.

15. Nashville *Union*, April–August 1862; Knoxville *Register*, April 1862–July 1863; Chattanooga *Rebel*, September 1862–July 1863; ER-1863, 3; Genovese, *Roll, Jordan, Roll*, 648, 798.

16. Cartmell Diary, August 14, 1862; Bills Diary, July 30, 1862; Porter Diary, August 10, 1862; Jesse Cox Diary, April 17, 1862, TSLA; ER-1863, 12–14; William J. Simmons, *Men of Mark* (Cleveland, 1887), 362.

17. Indiana Yearly Meeting's Executive Committee for the Relief of Colored Freedmen, *Report* (Richmond, Ind., 1864), 58; Cartmell Diary, June 7, 1863; Bills Diary, September 2, 1862, June 1–9, 1863; Porter Diary, August 13, 1863, December 16, 1864; ER-1863, 12.

18. Wilbur F. Hinman, *The Story of the Sherman Brigade* (Alliance, Ohio, 1897), 260; Bills Diary, October 20, 25, 1862; Knox, *Slave and Freeman*, 52 (quoted); Frank R. Levstick, ed., "A Journey among the Contrabands: The Diary of Walter Totten Carpenter," *Indiana Magazine of History*, LXXIII (September 1977), 216; Laura J. Haviland, *A Woman's Life Work* (5th ed., Grand Rapids, Mich., 1881), 264.

19. ER-1863, 12–13; Mrs. De Moville testimony, 56, AFIC; Knox, *Slave and Freeman*, 48; Trimble, ed., "Behind the Lines," 70–71 (quoted); Edward P. Williams, *Extracts from Letters to ABT* (New York, 1903), 46 (quoted).

20. Knox, *Slave and Freeman*, 58–62; J. B. Killebrew, "Recollections of my Life" (2 vols., 1896–97, typescript at TSLA), I, 184–85; Bills Diary, October 23, 1862, September 22, 24, 1863; Matthews Diary, July 30, August 1, 1864, February 2, 1865.

21. Amanda McDowell, *Fiddles in the Cumberlands*, ed. by Lela McDowell Blankenship (New York, 1945), 227; Bills Diary, August 21, September 24, October 17, 1863; Trimble, ed., "Behind the

Lines," 62–63, 78–79; Wiley, *Southern Negroes,* 76; Ann Fentress to Andrew Johnson, November 5, 1864, Andrew Johnson Papers, Library of Congress; Simmons, *Men of Mark,* 241.

22. Trimble, ed., "Behind the Lines," 78–79; Cartmell Diary, March 12, June 16, 1863; Bills Diary, September 22, October 14, 1864; Porter Diary, May 7, 28, June 25, 1864; W. Bosson to Lorenzo Thomas, January 27, 1864, LR by Adjutant General L. Thomas Relating to Colored Troops, RG 94, NA; Louisville *Journal,* February 4, 1864.

23. George L. Stearns testimony, 57, AFIC; Mary Reynolds to Simeon Reynolds, February 10, 1864, Reynolds Papers; Cartmell Diary, November 13, 1862, July 14, 1863, February 21, 1864; Bills Diary, August 15, 1862, September 24, October 17, 1863 (quoted), January 28, 1865 (quoted).

24. *AS,* XVIII, 307; Quarles, *Negro in the Civil War,* 53; Edmund Kirke [pseudonym for James R. Gilmore], *Down in Tennessee and Back by Way of Richmond* (New York, 1865), 170–71 (quoted).

25. Belle Edmondson Diary, February 15, 1864, SHC; Memphis *Avalanche,* June 11, 1862; Mary Reynolds to Simeon Reynolds, February 16, 1864, Reynolds Papers; Nashville *Press,* February 6, 1865; Samuel Henderson Diary, March 31, 1863, TSLA; New York *National Antislavery Standard,* August 29, 1863.

26. James L. Roark, *Masters without Slaves: Southern Planters in the Civil War and Reconstruction* (New York, 1977), 86–90; Bills Diary, September 25, 1863; Mrs. De Moville testimony, 56, AFIC; Henry Craft Diary, February 8, 29, 1864, SHC.

27. Killebrew, "Recollections," I, 184, 187–90; Memphis *Bulletin,* May 11, 1865; Cartmell Diary, March 12, 1863; New York *Tribune,* April 30, 1864; Nashville *Dispatch,* May 6, 1864.

28. Roark, *Masters without Slaves,* 94–96; Armstrong, *Old Massa's People,* 301–02; Powers, *Pencilings,* 116–18; *AS,* XVIII, 16.

29. Powers, *Pencilings,* 71, 116; Levi Coffin, *Reminiscences* (Cincinnati, 1876), 634; Rose, *Rehearsal for Reconstruction,* 20; Quarles, *Negro in the Civil War,* 46; Knox, *Slave and Freeman,* 57; Cincinnati *Gazette,* March 24, 1862 (quoted).

30. *AS,* XVIII, 591; W. B. Lewis to George A. Washington, March 6, 1863, Washington Papers.

31. Sarah Kennedy to David Kennedy, December 22, 1862, Kennedy Papers; Bills Diary, January 1, 1863; Benjamin F. McGee, *History of the 72d Indiana Volunteer Infantry*, ed. by William R. Jewell (La Fayette, Ind., 1882), 125; Wiley, *Southern Negroes*, 18; W. D. Bickham, *Rosecrans' Campaign* (Cincinnati, 1863), 115–16.

32. W. B. Lewis to George A. Washington, March 6, 1863, Washington Papers; *AS*, VII, 28; XVIII, 76; Mary Reynolds to Simeon Reynolds, February 16, May 1, 1864, Reynolds Papers; Isaac Lane, *Autobiography* (Nashville, 1916), 51; Wiley, *Southern Negroes*, 108.

33. *AS*, XVI, Tenn. sec., 9, 25; Powers, *Pencilings*, 71; Pennsylvania Freedmen's Relief Association, *Report of the Proceedings of a Meeting Held at Concert Hall* (Philadelphia, 1863), 7.

34. Mitchell, ed., "Confederate Surgeon," 80–81; James T. Shields to an uncle, November 2, 1863, Shields Family Papers, McClung Collection Library, Knoxville.

35. When the table 2 sample counties are used, the average prices for slaves between twelve and forty years old are $621.25 for eight males and $615.10 for ten females. The deed books with these entries were from Carroll, Davidson, Henry, Jefferson, Madison, and Montgomery counties.

36. *AS*, XVI, Tenn. sec., 1, XVIII, 183; William Truesdail to Andrew Johnson, February 16, 1863, Johnson Papers; U.S. Navy Department, *Official Records of the Union and Confederate Navies in the War of the Rebellion* (31 vols., Washington, 1894–1927), ser. 1, XXIII, 339.

37. Cincinnati *Gazette*, November 13, 1862; Philadelphia *Christian Recorder*, December 27, 1862; Coffin, *Reminiscences*, 630; Jane Washington to George A. Washington, [March 1864], Washington Papers; Maury County Minute Book, XIV, 234; *AS*, XVIII, 81.

38. Porter Diary, August 17, 1863, May 26, 1864; *OR*, ser. 1, XVII, pt. 2, 201; A. A. Smith, G.O. 3, November 29, 1863, vol. 171/208–DMT, 2, RG 393, NA; M. N. Puckett to Clinton B. Fisk, January 15, 1866, Reports of Outrages, Riots and Murders Received by the Asst. Commissioner for Ky. and Tenn., RG 105, NA; *AS*, supp. ser. 1, VIII, 1084; French Diary, December 14, 1864; Memphis *Bulletin*, March 4, 1865; Nashville *Times and True Union*, February 20, 1865.

39. Nashville *Dispatch*, July 28, 1863; Cartmell Diary, May 23, 1863; Porter Diary, May 16, 1864; Fanny Woods Diary, February 25, 1864, SHC; Graf and Haskins, eds., *Johnson Papers*, V, 510–11, VI, 319.

40. William P. Lyon to William W. Michael, July 3, 1863, vol. 172/214–DMT, 82–84, RG 393, NA; *AS*, supp. ser. 1, V, 315; Martha Luttrell Mitchell Memoir, 1, TSLA; *AS*, XVIII, 253 (quoted).

41. James H. Otey Diary, October 7, 1862, SHC; Craft Diary, December 7, 1863; Barker Diary, February 5, 1864; Bills Diary, November 5, 1862; A. A. Smith to B. H. Polk, April 20, 1864, vol. 170/205–DMT, 26, RG 393, NA.

42. Coffin, *Reminiscences*, 634; Cartmell Diary, August 19, 1862, April 19, June 12, 1863. Also see Trimble, ed., "Behind the Lines," 65; L. Maria Child, ed., *The Freedmen's Book* (Boston, 1865), 265–67; Philadelphia *Christian Recorder*, December 27, 1862; and Mary Reynolds to Simeon Reynolds, January 6, June 20, 1864, Reynolds Papers.

43. Clinton B. Fisk to Oliver O. Howard, September 2, 1865, Tenn. vol. 15, 55, RG 105, NA; Davis Tillson to W. T. Clarke, August 18, 1865, and W. T. Clarke to Clinton B. Fisk, August 10, 1865, Registered LR by the Asst. Commissioner for Ky. and Tenn., RG 105, NA; William B. Gaw to G. M. Bascom, November 6, 1865, LR by the District of East Tennessee, RG 393, NA; *OR*, ser. 3, V, 13, 662. The August figures for Memphis and Nashville may include a few blacks who had lived in contraband camps in June. All the urban figures include some loyal slaves, though most blacks in these towns were contrabands. See Alrutheus Ambush Taylor, *The Negro in Tennessee, 1865–1880* (Washington, 1941), 27.

Chapter 3

1. Graf and Haskins, eds., *Johnson Papers*, V, lxxi, 211; Miller, ed., "Dear Master," 91 (quoted).

2. *U.S. Statutes at Large*, XII, 1258; *Congressional Globe*, 37 Cong., 1 Sess., 223 (July 22, 1861), 257, 265 (July 25, 1861); Wiley, *Southern Negroes*, 175; *OR*, ser. 2, I, 761–62.

3. *U.S. Statutes at Large*, XII, 319, 354.

4. Quarles, *Negro in the Civil War*, 65; J. H. Hammond to Col. Worthington, July 11, 1862, William T. Sherman Letterbook B, 107, GPB (quoted); Nashville *Times*, March 3, 4, 1862; Cincinnati *Gazette*, March 3, 11, 1862; I. F. Quimby, G.O. 37, August 22, 1862, vol. 101/248A–DKY, 117, RG 393, NA.

5. *OR*, ser. 1, VII, 668, X, pt. 2, 15, 31, ser. 2, I, 778; Henry W. Halleck, G.O. 46, February 22, 1862, vol. 50/77–DMo, 161, RG 393, NA; Philadelphia *Press*, February 25, 1862; U.S. Navy Department, *Official Records of the Navies*, ser. 1, XXIII, 149. Early in the war, the army also followed an exclusion policy in Louisiana and Virginia but not along the Southeastern coast. See Louis S. Gerteis, *From Contraband to Freedman: Federal Policy toward Southern Blacks, 1861–1865* (Westport, Conn., 1973), 13, 30, 51, 67; and Quarles, *Negro in the Civil War*, 65.

6. Nashville *Times*, March 14, 1862; Cincinnati *Gazette*, March 15, 1862; Shelbyville *News*, June 21, 1862; Memphis *Avalanche*, June 8–13, 1862; Nashville *Union*, April 20, August 3, 1862.

7. *OR*, ser. 1, VII, 668; New York *Tribune*, February 22, 1862; Channing Richards, "Dealing with Slavery," in Military Order of the Loyal Legion of the United States, Ohio Commandery, *Sketches of War History 1861–1865* (7 vols., Cincinnati, 1888–1910), IV, 318–21; Graf and Haskins, eds., *Johnson Papers*, VI, 88–89.

8. Henry W. Halleck, Special Field Order 21, April 22, 1862, vol. 89/?–16AC, 7, RG 393, NA; Simon, ed., *Grant Papers*, V, 86–87; Bobby L. Lovett, "Nashville's Fort Negley: A Symbol of Blacks' Involvement with the Union Army," *Tennessee Historical Quarterly*, XLI (Spring 1982), 8; Wright, *Eighth Kentucky*, 71.

9. John Beatty, *Citizen Soldier* (Cincinnati, 1879), 117, 124. Expulsion orders usually did not explicitly require the return of slaves to masters but often produced that effect in violation of the law's spirit.

10. Byron R. Abernethy, ed., *Private Elisha Stockwell, Jr. Sees the Civil War* (Norman, Okla., 1958), 25–26, 39; Dornblaser, *Sabre Strokes*, 120–21; Richards, "Dealing with Slavery," 324–25; Bell Irwin Wiley, *The Life of Billy Yank: The Common Soldier of the Union Army* (Indianapolis, 1951), 115–16.

11. William P. Sipes, *Seventh Pennsylvania Veteran Volunteer Cavalry* (Pottsville, Pa., 1905), 14–15; Chicago *Tribune*, July 19,

1862; Charles W. Wills, *The Life of an Illinois Soldier* (Washington, 1906), 166–67, 177 (quoted).

12. Simon, ed., *Grant Papers,* IV, 438; Chicago *Tribune,* July 15, 1862; Theodore C. Blegen, ed., *The Civil War Letters of Colonel Hans Christian Heg* (Northfield, Minn., 1936), 79; Stephen Z. Starr, *Jennison's Jayhawkers: A Civil War Cavalry Regiment and Its Commander* (Baton Rouge, 1973), 173–82; Edgar Langsdorf and R. W. Richmond, eds., "Letters of Daniel R. Anthony, 1857–1862," *Kansas Historical Quarterly,* XXIV (Winter 1958), 458–65.

13. *U.S. Statutes at Large,* XII, 591; Simon, ed., *Grant Papers,* V, xxiv, 311.

14. Grenville M. Dodge to George E. Bryant, September 3, 1862, vol. 32–16AC, 81, RG 393, NA; I. F. Quimby, G.O. 37, August 22, 1862, vol. 101/248–DKy, 117, RG 393, NA; W. W. Lowe, G.O. 3, September 5, 1862, vol. 172/217–DMT, 199, RG 393, NA; M. K. Lawler, S.O. 76, November 14, 1862, vol. 88–16AC, 313, RG 393, NA; *OR,* ser. 1, XVII, pt. 1, 470–71; U.S. Navy Department, *Official Records of the Navies,* ser. 1, XXIII, 345, 449.

15. Union Citizens of Memphis Petition, [1862], B. W. Sharp to Andrew Johnson, October 11, 1862, and William Truesdail to Andrew Johnson, February 16, 1863, Johnson Papers; Nashville *Dispatch,* November 26, December 11, 1862; Memphis *Bulletin,* August 15, 1862; *OR,* ser. 1, XVII, pt. 2, 295, XXIII, pt. 2, 17–18.

16. McGee, *72d Indiana Infantry,* 226 (quoted); William P. Lyon to C. Goddard, July 13, 1863, vol. 172/214–DMT, 88, RG 393, NA; L. Thomas to W. S. Rosecrans, June 15, 1863, LR by the Department of the Cumberland, RG 393, NA; *OR,* ser. 3, III, 559 (quoted).

17. Francis F. McKinney, *Education in Violence: The Life of George H. Thomas and the History of the Army of the Cumberland* (Detroit, 1961), 82–83, 272; *OR,* ser. 3, IV, 770–71; William D. Whipple to L. H. Rousseau, February 3, 1864, LR by the District of Middle Tennessee, RG 393, NA; Grenville M. Dodge to H. R. Mizner, January 23, 1864, vol. 32–16AC, 349, RG 393, NA.

18. John Eaton to S. S. Jocelyn, May 18, 1863, AMA (quoted); *OR,* ser. 3, III, 100; *Senate Executive Documents,* 38 Cong., 2 Sess., No. 28, 1–2.

19. Phelps Paine to Mr. Shoecroft, September 22, 1863, Walton

Family Papers, Joint University Library, Nashville; Millon Curran, order, September 12, 1864, David Campbell Papers, Duke University Library, Durham, N.C.; Jane Washington to George A. Washington, [March 1864], Washington Papers; Trimble, ed., "Behind the Lines," 63; F. Copeland to George L. Stearns, March 5, 1864, LR by the Colored Troops Division, RG 94, NA; Charles Aldrich, "Incidents Connected with the History of the Thirty-Second Iowa Infantry," *Iowa Journal of History and Politics,* IV (January 1906), 84.

20. By 1863 the federal occupation of Tennessee was organized into three major district commands, one for each region of the state.

21. Nashville *Press,* February 20, 1864; R. D. Mussey to A. B. Morse, July 8, 1864, vol. 220/227–DC, 204, RG 393, NA; R. D. Mussey to Lorenzo Thomas, February 28, 1864, LR by Adjutant General L. Thomas Relating to Colored Troops, RG 94, NA; *Senate Executive Documents,* 38 Cong., 2 Sess., No. 28, 11, 16–18.

22. *Senate Executive Documents,* 38 Cong., 2 Sess., No. 28, 17–18. For proof of the post commander's guilt, see Porter Diary, September 6, 1863; and Simmons, *Men of Mark,* 241.

23. *OR,* ser. 2, VI, 210; Grenville M. Dodge to George E. Bryant, September 3, 1862, vol. 32–16AC, 81, RG 393, NA; J. A. Garfield to William P. Lyon, June 17, 1863, and Joseph L. Murray to A. A. Smith, November 11, 1863, LR by the Post of Nashville, RG 393, NA. Examples of freedom papers appear in vol. 12–DET, 348, vol. 118–DC, 243–44, 246, 309, RG 393, NA.

24. Nashville *Press,* February 8 (quoted), July 7, August 15, 1864; Coffin, *Reminiscences,* 633–34.

25. Memphis *Argus,* July 17, October 15, 1862; Nashville *Dispatch,* July 27, August 15, September 4, November 8, December 16, 1862, February 14, 1863.

26. *OR,* ser. 1, XVII, pt. 2, 295, 863–64; John Sherman to William T. Sherman, August 24, 1862, and William T. Sherman to John Sherman, September 3, October 1, 1862, William T. Sherman Papers, Library of Congress; William T. Sherman to J. J. Gant, September 23, 1862, Sherman Letterbook C, 144, GPB; *U.S. Statutes at Large,* XII, 1267 (quoted).

27. Memphis *Bulletin,* November 12–13, 1862, February 11, 1863; J. T. Swayne to William T. Sherman, November 14, 1862, Sher-

man Papers; William T. Sherman to B. W. Sharp, November 14, 1862, Sherman Letterbook M, 61, GPB; *OR*, ser. 1, XVII, pt. 2, 865.

28. Memphis *Bulletin*, October 24, December 3, 1862, January 31, March 4, May 7, 1863, May 15, 18, 1864; Memphis Board of Mayor and Aldermen, Journal, vol. for August 1862–June 1866, 168, 262–75, City Hall, Memphis. Clifton R. Hall, *Andrew Johnson, Military Governor of Tennessee* (Princeton, N.J., 1916), 137–38, accepts the *Bulletin*'s charge as true, but the official city record belies it.

29. Nashville *Union*, February 17, 1863; Nashville *Dispatch*, February 13, 14, 22, 1863.

30. Nashville *Dispatch*, February 22, March 3, April 30, June 24, 25, July 10, 1863.

31. Ibid., October 20, 1863; Nashville *Union*, December 9, 1863 (quoted).

32. Proceedings of the trial of James Andrews, June 8, 1864, Court Martial Records, RG 153, NA; L. H. Rousseau, G.O. 36, August 6, 1864, vol. 9–DMT, 65–66, RG 393, NA.

33. Nashville *Times and True Union*, September 12, October 7, 1864. The Tennessee *Code* (1858) says nothing about a judge's power to overrule a verdict, but, because no proslavery newspaper challenged the action's legality, precedents may have existed. For clashes over the slave code in other occupied areas, see Gerteis, *Contraband*, 31; John W. Blassingame, *Black New Orleans, 1860–1880* (Chicago, 1973), 31–33.

34. Joseph Warren, ed., *Extracts from Documents in the Office of the General Superintendent of Refugees and Freedmen* (Memphis, 1865), 11; Daniel Chapman to ed. of *American Missionary*, December 9, 1863, AMA; Indiana Freedmen's Aid Commission, *Report of the Board of Managers* (Indianapolis, 1864), 28; Pompey MacDonald to N. J. T. Dana, December 21, 1865, Unregistered LR by the Memphis Subassistant Commissioner, RG 105, NA.

35. R. L. Nichol to Andrew Johnson, October 21, 1864, Johnson Papers; Nashville *Republican Banner*, November 18, 1865; Nashville *Press*, March 8, 1865; Memphis *Argus*, June 10, 1864; Nashville *Dispatch*, June 23, 1863, August 18, 1864. Federal military courts in Louisiana commonly heard black testimony. See Ripley, *Slaves and Freedmen*, 101.

36. Thomas B. Johnson to Andrew Johnson, August 8, 1863, Johnson Papers.

Chapter 4

1. ER-1863, 15; Chattanooga *Rebel*, June 28, 1863; Lyman Abbott, *Reminiscences* (New York, 1923), 249; Bills Diary, August 28, 1862; Porter Diary, August 29, 1863.

2. Statements by William Lea (November 17, 1865), William H. Lea (October 19, 1865), and Albert Lea (December 16, 1865), Affidavits and Statements filed with the Memphis Provost Marshal of Freedmen, RG 105, NA; E. P. Burton, *Diary* (Des Moines, 1939), 6; Pennsylvania Freedmen's Relief Association, *Report of a Meeting*, 7; Nashville *Union*, February 9, 1864; Levstik, ed., "Contrabands," 215.

3. J. P. Bardwell to M. E. Strieby, December 13, 1864, AMA; Levstik, ed., "Contrabands," 216; Pennsylvania Freedmen's Relief Association, *Report of a Meeting*, 7; *Pennsylvania Freedmen's Bulletin*, I (February 1865), 14; *OR*, ser. 1, XXIV, pt. 3, 149.

4. *OR*, ser. 1, XXIV, pt. 3, 149; Levstik, ed., "Contrabands," 210; Nashville *Press*, August 26, 1864; Friends' Association of Philadelphia and Its Vicinity for the Relief of Colored Freedmen, *Statistics of the Operation of the Executive Board* (Philadelphia, 1864), 11; Joseph Warren, ed., *Extracts from the Reports of Superintendents of Freedmen* (Vicksburg, Miss., 1864), ser. 2, 23.

5. Sarah Kennedy to David Kennedy, February 20, 1864, Kennedy Papers; Lyman W. Ayer to M. E. Strieby, February 18, 1865, AMA; *Pennsylvania Freedmen's Bulletin*, I (February 1865), 14–15; W. B. Dortch to B. H. Polk, June 13, 1865, LR by the District of Middle Tennessee, RG 393, NA; Memphis *Bulletin* clipping enclosed with William Wallace to Andrew Johnson, September 2, 1865, Registered LR by the Asst. Commissioner for Ky. and Tenn., RG 105, NA; Cincinnati *Colored Citizen*, November 7, 1863.

6. Berlin, *Slaves Without Masters*, 253, 381–86; Joseph Warren, ed., *Reports Relating to Colored Schools in Mississippi, Arkansas, and Western Tennessee* (Memphis, 1865), 24; ER-1863, 40; Nashville

Dispatch, December 27, 1862, April 9, 1863; Nashville *Press,* May 11, 1863; Memphis *Bulletin,* December 22, 1863.

7. *OR,* ser. 1, XXIV, pt. 3, 149; Indiana Freedmen's Aid Commission, *Report,* 31; Memphis *Bulletin,* October 25, 1862, May 17, September 1, 1864; Edward H. East to the provost marshal, August 19, 1864, vol. 174/224–DMT, 107, RG 393, NA; excerpts from the J. G. McKee Diary in R. W. McGranahan, ed., *Historical Sketch of the Freedmen's Missions of the United Presbyterian Church, 1862–1904* (Knoxville, 1904), 10–11, 16.

8. ER-1864, 4 (quoted); John M. Palmer, *Personal Recollections: The Story of an Earnest Life* (Cincinnati, 1901), 118.

9. *OR,* ser. 1, XVII, pt. 1, 470–71, 481, LII, pt. 1, 301–02, 323, ser. 3, II, 569, 663; John Eaton, *Grant, Lincoln, and the Freedmen: Reminiscences of the Civil War* (New York, 1907), 13; Gerteis, *Contraband,* 15, 20, 30, 51–52.

10. Eaton, *Grant, Lincoln, and the Freedmen,* x–xvi; ER-1863, 21, 45; ER-1864, 92; John Eaton to C. B. Boynton, September 11, 1863, Mississippi vol. 74, 67, RG 105, NA.

11. Eaton, *Grant, Lincoln, and the Freedmen,* 22, 25–27; John N. Waddell Diary, November 23, 1862, Library of Congress; ER-1863, 53.

12. Eaton, *Grant, Lincoln, and the Freedmen,* 30–32; Cincinnati *Gazette,* February 3, 1863; James E. Yeatman, *A Report on the Condition of the Freedmen of the Mississippi* (St. Louis, 1864), 1; ER-1863, 40; Coffin, *Reminiscences,* 629.

13. Eaton to ?, March 13, 1863, AMA; Friends' Association of Philadelphia, *Statistics,* 11.

14. Cartmell Diary, June 7, 1863; Bills Diary, June 1–9, September 12, 1863; John Phillips, Consolidated Report, February 1, 1864, LR by Adjutant General L. Thomas Relating to Colored Troops, RG 94, NA; *OR,* ser. 1, XXXII, pt. 1, 525, 616; *Senate Committee Reports,* 38 Cong., 1 Sess., No. 63, 86; Warren, ed., *Extracts from Reports,* ser. 2, 46.

15. John Eaton to Col. Smith, May 22, 1863, Mississippi vol. 74, 54, RG 105, NA; T. A. Walker to A. G. Tuther, October 26, 1864, LR by the District of Memphis, RG 393, NA; T. A. Walker to Davis Tillson, July 8, 1865, Unregistered LR by the Memphis Subassistant

Commissioner, RG 105, NA; T. A. Walker to I. G. Kappner, November 12, 1864, LR by Fort Pickering, RG 393, NA; Joseph Warren, ed., *Final Report of the Freedmen Schools in the Department Lately under the Supervision of Colonel John Eaton, Jr.* (Vicksburg, 1865), 5. In *Grant, Lincoln, and the Freedmen*, 163, Eaton claims incorrectly that the President's Island camp had been highly successful.

16. Graf and Haskins, ed., *Johnson Papers*, VI, 488–90; McKee Diary excerpts in McGranahan, ed., *Freedmen's Missions*, 14.

17. *OR*, ser. 1, XXXI, pt. 3, 198, ser. 3, IV, 770; *Senate Executive Documents*, 38 Cong., 2 Sess., No. 28, 10; Horatio Van Cleve, S.O. 31, December 26, 1863, vol. 63/87–DMT, 184, RG 393, NA; William P. Lyon to C. Goddard, July 13, 1863, vol. 172/214–DMT, 88, RG 393, NA.

18. *OR*, ser. 3, IV, 770; *AS*, XIX, 206; Graf and Haskins, eds., *Johnson Papers*, VI, 489.

19. *OR*, ser. 3, IV, 771; Levstik, ed., "Contrabands," 220.

20. *Senate Executive Documents*, 38 Cong., 2 Sess., No. 28, 2; A. A. Smith to B. H. Polk, February 18, 1864, vol. 170/205–DMT, 14, RG 393, NA; R. D. Mussey to George Mason, April 4, 1864, LR by Adjutant General L. Thomas Relating to Colored Troops, RG 94, NA; R. W. Barnard to R. D. Mussey, October 11, 1864, LR by the Colored Troops Division, RG 94, NA. Patton, *Unionism*, 147, gives an incorrect account of the camp system's beginning.

21. *Senate Executive Documents*, 38 Cong., 2 Sess., No. 28, 3–5; R. W. Barnard to Oliver O. Howard, May 30, 1865, Registered LR by the Asst. Commissioner for Ky. and Tenn., RG 105, NA; Western Freedmen's Aid Commission, *Second Annual Report* (Cincinnati, 1865), 28.

22. *Freedmen's Bulletin*, I (March 1865), 77–78; Nashville *Press*, December 2, 1864; *Freedmen's Friend*, I (February 1865), 26–27; *National Freedman*, I (May 1865), 127; Indiana Yearly Meeting's Committee for Freedmen, *Report*, 53; R. D. Mussey to C. P. Brown, January 23, 1865, LR by Adjutant General L. Thomas Relating to Colored Troops, RG 393, NA.

23. Cincinnati *Gazette*, February 17, 1864; R. D. Mussey to T. J. Morgan, April 26, 1864, vol. 220/227–DC, 81, RG 393, NA; Chattanooga *Gazette*, December 7, 11, 1864.

24. Sources for table 4, listed by column, are: (1) John Eaton to ?, March 13, 1863, AMA; (2) Yeatman, *Report*, 2–4; Toledo *Blade*, October 30, 1863; (3) John Phillips, Consolidated Report, February 1, 1864, and R. D. Mussey to George Mason, March 28, 1864, LR by Adjutant General L. Thomas Relating to Colored Troops, RG 94, NA; Indiana Freedmen's Aid Commission, *Report*, 18; Levstik, ed., "Contrabands," 210, 221; (4) Warren, ed., *Extracts from Reports*, ser. 1, 3; Indiana Yearly Meeting's Committee for Freedmen, *Report*, 57; John C. Starkweather to B. H. Polk, May 25, 1864, vol. 166/191–DMT (unpaginated), RG 393, NA; (5) Memphis *Bulletin*, July 6, 1864; *Senate Executive Documents*, 38 Cong., 2 Sess., No. 28, 11; (6) T. A. Walker to A. G. Tuther, October 26, 1864, LR by the District of Memphis, RG 393, NA; Indiana Freedmen's Aid Commission, *Report*, 28, 30; R. W. Barnard to R. D. Mussey, September 25, 1864, LR by the Colored Troops Division, RG 94, NA; (7) *Friends Review*, XVIII (April 29, 1865), 555–57; *Freedmen's Friend*, I (February 1865), 27; (8) Abbott, *Reminiscences*, 250; Richard J. Hinton to W. T. Clarke, July 31, 1865, Registered LR by the Asst. Commissioner for Ky. and Tenn., RG 105, NA; (9) Superintendents of Freedmen for the State of Arkansas and the District of West Tennessee, *Reports* (Memphis, 1865), 13; Richard J. Hinton to W. T. Clark, July 31, 1865, Registered LR by the Asst. Commissioner for Ky. and Tenn., RG 105, NA; *National Freedman*, I (May 1865), 127; (10) R. W. Barnard, Consolidated Report for June 1865, Registered LR by the Asst. Commissioner for Ky. and Tenn., RG 105, NA.

25. Nashville *Tennessean*, August 16, 1936 (supplement).

26. Convention of Freedmen's Commissions, *Minutes* (Cincinnati, 1864), passim; Ronald E. Butchart, *Northern Schools, Southern Blacks, and Reconstruction: Freedmen's Education, 1862–1875* (Westport, Conn., 1980), 68; Cincinnati *Colored Citizen*, November 7, 1863; Nashville *Times and True Union*, December 31, 1864; A. L. Chetlain et al., "To the Benevolent and Philanthropic Friends of Freedmen" (handbill, 1865), AMA. Eaton sent his own fundraisers into the North. See John Eaton to Robert W. Carroll, June 27, 1863, Mississippi vol. 74, 63–64, RG 105, NA.

27. ER-1863, 4, 30; Western Freedmen's Aid Commission, *Appeal in Behalf of the National Freedmen* (Cincinnati, 1864), 5; L. Thomas, S.O. 28, May 20, 1863, L. Thomas Orders and Letters Book,

vol. for April–November 1863, 62, GPB; L. Thomas, Order 15, March 28, 1864, L. Thomas Special Orders of Appointment Book, 105, GPB.

28. Indiana Freedmen's Aid Commission, *Report*, 18, 28, 31; Pennsylvania Freedmen's Relief Association, *Report of a Meeting*, 7; Western Freedmen's Aid Commission, *Second Annual Report*, 29; Association of Friends for the Aid and Elevation of the Freedmen, *Report* (Philadelphia, 1865), 18; undated McKee Diary excerpt in McGranahan, ed., *Freedmen's Missions*, 15 (quoted).

29. ER-1864, 87; *Freedmen's Bulletin*, I (March 1865), 78; Indiana Freedmen's Aid Commission, *Report*, 30; Abbott, *Reminiscences*, 248; R. W. Barnard to Oliver O. Howard, May 30, 1865, Registered LR by the Asst. Commissioner for Ky. and Tenn., RG 105, NA.

30. James McNeal, "Biographical Sketch of Reverend Joseph G. McKee, the Pioneer Missionary to the Freedmen in Nashville, Tennessee," in McGranahan, ed., *Freedmen's Missions*, 10–11; Coffin, *Reminiscences*, 632; *Senate Executive Documents*, 38 Cong., 2 Sess., No. 28, 6; P. H. Clemons to R. D. Mussey, May 31, 1864, vol. 223/431–DC, 106, RG 105, NA.

31. William T. Alderson, ed., "The Civil War Reminiscences of John Johnson, 1861–1865," *Tennessee Historical Quarterly*, XIV (March 1955), 52; Burton, *Diary*, 8.

32. Cincinnati *Gazette*, January 29, 1863; ER-1863, 5; Coffin, *Reminiscences*, 629; *Senate Executive Documents*, 38 Cong., 2 Sess., No. 28, 11; Indiana Freedmen's Aid Commission, *Report*, 53, 57; Levstik, ed., "Contrabands," 210.

33. Abbott, *Reminiscences*, 248–50; Indiana Freedmen's Aid Commission, *Report*, 18; Yeatman, *Report*, 1–4, 15; R. W. Barnard to Oliver O. Howard, May 30, 1865, Registered LR by the Asst. Commissioner for Ky. and Tenn., RG 105, NA; Burton, *Diary*, 8; *Senate Executive Documents*, 38 Cong., 2 Sess., No. 28, 11; Indiana Yearly Meeting's Committee for Freedmen, *Report*, 52.

34. Wiley, *Billy Yank*, 224; ER-1863, 30; John Eaton to Capt. Dockson, [March 1863], Mississippi vol. 74, 35, RG 105, NA; U. S. Grant, G.O. 7, November 17, 1862, vol. 13/21–DT, 15, RG 393, NA.

35. *OR*, ser. 3, IV, 44–45; L. Thomas, Order 4, February 8, 1864, L. Thomas Special Orders of Appointment Book, 38–39, GPB; L.

Thomas to Edwin M. Stanton, February 21, 1864, L. Thomas Orders and Letters Book, vol. for November 1863–July 1864, 37, RG 94, NA.

36. ER-1863, 5; *Senate Executive Documents*, 38 Cong., 2 Sess., No. 28, 6; William T. Sherman, G.O. 8, April 19, 1864, vol. 14/20– MDM, 25, RG 393, NA.

37. *OR*, ser. 1, XXXI, pt. 3, 198; Indiana Freedmen's Aid Commission, *Report*, 19, 28; Coffin, *Reminiscences*, 628; Burton, *Diary*, 8; Convention of Freedmen's Commissions, *Minutes*, 16; R. W. Barnard to Oliver O. Howard, May 30, 1865, Registered LR by the Asst. Commissioner for Ky. and Tenn., RG 105, NA.

38. Pennsylvania Freedmen's Relief Association, *Report of a Meeting*, 7; Cincinnati *Colored Citizen*, November 7, 1863.

39. ER-1863, 7; Hughes, *Thirty Years*, 193; Coffin, *Reminiscences*, 631–32; *Senate Executive Documents*, 38 Cong., 2 Sess., No. 28, 9–11; Indiana Freedmen's Aid Commission, *Report*, 23; *OR*, ser. 3, IV, 772; Warren, ed., *Extracts from Reports*, ser. 2, 40; *Friends Review*, XVII (January 23, 1864), 322.

40. *U.S. Statutes at Large*, XII, 645, XIII, 23, 120–30; ER-1864, 96; Charles C. Lee to D. O. McCord, December 3, 1864, LR by the Medical Director, Mississippi Records, RG 105, NA; L. Thomas, Order 1, January 1, 1865, L. Thomas Special Orders of Appointment Book, 320, GPB; L. Thomas to E. D. Townsend, March 27, 1865, L. Thomas Letterbook, vol. for July 1864–June 1865, 158–59, GPB.

41. Yeatman, *Report*, 4; Warren, ed., *Extracts from Reports*, ser. 2, 44; J. A. Grove to W. T. Clark, September 21, 1865 (quoted), Registered LR by the Asst. Commissioner for Ky. and Tenn., RG 105, NA; William E. Strong to Oliver O. Howard, July 5, 1865, Unregistered LR by the Memphis Subassistant Commissioner, RG 105, NA; R. D. Mussey to Lorenzo Thomas, February 24, 1864, LR by Adjutant General L. Thomas Relating to Colored Troops, RG 94, NA.

42. Indiana Yearly Meeting's Committee for Freedmen, *Report*, 58; Knox, *Slave and Freeman*, 57.

Chapter 5

1. New York *Times*, January 17, 1864; Webber, *Deep Like the Rivers*, 140–42.

2. Peter Maslowski, *Treason Must Be Made Odious: Military Occupation and Wartime Reconstruction in Nashville, Tennessee, 1862–1865* (Millwood, N.Y., 1978), 116.

3. George L. Stearns testimony, 59, 62, 67, AFIC; Pennsylvania Freedmen's Relief Association, *Report of a Meeting*, 8–9; R. D. Mussey to Joseph Parrish, March 27, 1864 (quoted), vol. 220/227–DC, 36, RG 393, NA; R. D. Mussey, circular, December 9, 1864, Records of Capt. R. D. Mussey, RG 393, NA.

4. L. Thomas to Edwin M. Stanton, November 16, 1863, L. Thomas Letters and Orders Book, vol. for April–November 1863, 206, GPB; Indiana Freedmen's Aid Commission, *Report*, 19 (quoted), 26, 29; ER-1863, 38, 42–46 (quoted). Also see Robert F. Engs, *Freedom's First Generation: Black Hampton, Virginia, 1861–1890* (Philadelphia, 1979), 60–65.

5. Herman Belz, *Emancipation and Equal Rights: Politics and Constitutionalism in the Civil War Era* (New York, 1978), 62–72; Rose, *Rehearsal for Reconstruction*, 217–29; Ripley, *Slaves and Freedmen*, 88.

6. Genovese, *Roll, Jordan, Roll*, 273–74.

7. Sarah Kennedy to David Kennedy, September 13, 1863, February 20, 1865, Kennedy Papers; Craft Diary, June 29, July 17, August 31, 1863; Nashville *Press*, August 6, 1864; Warren, ed., *Extracts from Reports*, ser. 2, 23; George L. Stearns testimony, 67, AFIC.

8. Mackey Woods, petition, December 12, 1865, Affidavits and Statements filed with the Provost Marshal of Freedmen at Memphis, RG 105, NA; Philadelphia *Christian Recorder*, December 27, 1862; Nashville *Press and Times*, August 4, 1865.

9. ER-1863, 16, 35–36.

10. Ibid., 14, 35; John Eaton to Robert W. Carroll, [March 1863] (quoted), Mississippi vol. 74, 25, RG 105, NA; John Eaton to John A. Rawlins, February 14, 1863, LR by Headquarters of the Army, RG 108, NA.

11. John Eaton to Robert W. Carroll, February 9, 1863, and John Eaton to Henry Wilson, [March 1863], Mississippi vol. 74, 14–15, 18, 22, RG 105, NA.

12. Levstik, "Contrabands," 221; ER-1863, 2, 52; Abbott, *Reminiscences*, 248; John Eaton to Joel Grant, September 3, 1863, Mis-

sissippi vol. 74, 71, RG 105, NA; R. D. Mussey to C. P. Brown, October 31, 1864, vol. 221–DC, 260, RG 393, NA.

13. Eaton, *Grant, Lincoln, and the Freedmen,* 58; Warren, ed., *Extracts from Reports,* ser. 1, 34, ser. 2, 24; "List of Colored Refugees from the State of Kentucky," vol. –/213–DMT, passim, RG 393, NA; Burton, *Diary,* 8; R. W. Barnard to Oliver O. Howard, May 30, 1865, Registered LR by the Asst. Commissioner for Ky. and Tenn., RG 105, NA; Charles H. Cole to Lorenzo Thomas, October 20, 1863, LR by the Colored Troops Divison, RG 94, NA.

14. L. Thomas, S.O. 94, November 5, 1863, L. Thomas Letters and Orders Book, vol. for April–November 1863, 197, GPB; Superintendents for the State of Arkansas and the District of West Tennessee, *Reports,* 13; Chicago *Tribune,* August 19, 1865; ER-1863, 45; Lewis Pettijohn to S. S. Jocelyn, March 8, 1864, AMA; Eaton, *Grant, Lincoln, and the Freedmen,* 27.

15. John Eaton to Henry Wilson, [March 1863], Mississippi vol. 74, 19, 21–22, RG 105, NA; Indiana Freedmen's Aid Commission, *Report,* 19.

16. Wiley, *Southern Negroes,* 341; McGee, *72d Indiana Infantry,* 226–27; Blegen, ed., *Heg Letters,* 170; Fitch, *Annals,* 619–20, 633; Porter Diary, July 4, 1864.

17. Charles F. Herndon, ed., *Some Comments Concerning Civil War Letters of an Ohio Family* (Fresno, Calif., 1959), 78 (quoted); George L. Stearns testimony, 58, AFIC; New York *National Antislavery Standard,* April 9, 1864; ER-1863, 10.

18. John Eaton to John A. Rawlins, February 14, 1863, LR by Headquarters of the Army, RG 108, NA; *U.S. Statutes at Large,* XII, 599; *OR,* ser. 1, XVII, pt. 2, 158–59; *Senate Executive Documents,* 38 Cong., 2 Sess., No. 28, 12; Yeatman, *Report,* 4. Less scrupulous federal officials on the Southeastern coastline began paying contraband laborers during the summer of 1862. See Gerteis, *Contraband,* 30, 54.

19. *OR,* ser. 1, XXIII, pt. 2, 17–18, 290–91, ser. 3, III, 560; George Burroughs to Andrew Johnson, October 8, 1863, and James St. C. Morton to Andrew Johnson, December 5, 1863, Johnson Papers.

20. *OR,* ser. 3, III, 840; George L. Stearns to Robert D. Owen,

November 24, 1863, 74, AFIC; R. D. Mussey to Whitlaw Reid, December 19, 1863, Appointment Commission's Personnel Branch file for Mussey, RG 94, NA; James St. C. Morton to Andrew Johnson, December 4, 1863, Johnson Papers; Alvan C. Gillem to A. A. Smith, October 1, 1863, LR by the Post of Nashville, RG 393, NA.

21. B. H. Polk to William T. Ward, December 16, 1863, and B. H. Polk to H. S. Granger, December 21, 1863, vol. 2–DMT, 43–44, 48, RG 393, NA; L. Howland to Hunter Brook, December 3, 1864, vol. 177/241–DMT, 245, RG 393, NA; R. D. Mussey to George Mason, April 11, 1864, Records of Capt. R. D. Mussey, RG 393, NA.

22. *Senate Executive Documents*, 38 Cong., 2 Sess., No. 28, 12–15; Yeatman, *Report*, 4; Fitch, *Annals*, 269–70.

23. ER-1863, 51; Memphis *Bulletin*, July 18, 21, 1863. Federals in New Orleans established a similar pass system. See Blassingame, *Black New Orleans*, 31.

24. Memphis *Bulletin*, August 8, 13, October 23, 1863, April 15, 1864; Warren, ed., *Extracts from Reports*, ser. 2, 23; L. Methundy to T. A. Walker, February 15, 1864, vol. 27/43–DWT, 151, RG 393, NA; Nashville *Dispatch*, April 10, 1864.

25. L. Thomas to George H. Thomas, February 27, 1864, L. Thomas Letters and Orders Book, vol. for November 1863–July 1864, 48, GPB; E. A. Paine, S.O. 11, May 30, 1863, vol. 168A–DMT, sec. 3, 97, RG 393, NA; Contract between Berry and Mary Taylor, January 26, 1864, Miscellaneous Records of the Superintendent at Lebanon, Tenn., RG 105, NA; *OR*, ser. 1, XXXII, pt. 2, 268–69 (quoted); E. A. Paine to B. H. Polk, January 26, 1864, LR by the Department of the Cumberland, RG 393, NA; W. D. Whipple to L. H. Rousseau, February 3, 1864, LR by the District of Middle Tennessee, RG 393, NA.

26. Wiley, *Southern Negroes*, 202–04, 211–12; Gerteis, *Contraband*, 150; *OR*, ser. 3, III, 100, 918; L. Thomas to Edwin M. Stanton, April 12, November 16, 1863, L. Thomas Letters and Orders Book, vol. for April–November 1863, 24–25, 206, GPB.

27. Eaton, *Grant, Lincoln, and the Freedmen*, 111; *Senate Executive Documents*, 38 Cong., 2 Sess., No. 28, 2; *OR*, ser. 3, IV, 124, 143, 166–67 (quoted).

28. Ripley, *Slaves and Freedmen*, 58, 205–06; *OR*, ser. 3, IV, 166–68.

29. John Eaton to Henry Wilson, [March 1863], and John Eaton to Henry Binmore, June 23, 1863, Mississippi vol. 74, 19–21, 47, 59, RG 105, NA; Eaton, *Grant, Lincoln, and the Freedmen*, 23–24; John Phillips, circular, December 30, 1863, U.S. Bureau of Refugees, Freedmen, and Abandoned Lands Orders and Circulars Collection, Memphis and Shelby County Library, Memphis.

30. A. D. Olds to G. Whipple, February 10, 1864, AMA; John Phillips, Consolidated Report, February 1, 1864, LR by Adjutant General L. Thomas Relating to Colored Troops, RG 94, NA; Memphis *Bulletin*, April 15, 1864; Nashville *Dispatch*, April 10, 1864.

31. R. D. Mussey to George Mason, April 11, 1864, LR by Adjutant General L. Thomas Relating to Colored Troops, RG 94, NA; Indiana Freedmen's Aid Commission, *Report*, 28; R. D. Mussey to Robert D. Owen, September 9, 1864, LR by the Colored Troops Division, RG 94, NA; West Tennessee File of Contracts, RG 105, NA.

32. Gerteis, *Contraband*, 155–56, 183–84.

33. Ibid., 181, 184; U.S. Census Office, *Eighth Census: Miscellaneous*, 512.

34. Warren, ed., *Extracts from Reports*, ser. 2, 25; C. C. Washburne, S.O. 209, November 28, 1864, vol. 13–DWT, 142, RG 393, NA; James Gilfillan, S.O. 43, December 22, 1864, vol. 186/200–DMT, 146, RG 393, NA; J. C. Starkweather, S.O. 96, October 12, 1864, vol. 167/193–DMT, 135–36, RG 393, NA.

35. *AS*, XIX, 214; Eaton, *Grant, Lincoln, and the Freedmen*, 207; Chicago *Tribune*, March 3, 1862; undated McKee Diary excerpts in McGranahan, ed., *Freedmen's Missions*, 15 (quoted).

36. "List of Colored Refugees from the State of Kentucky," vol. –/213–DMT, passim, RG 393, NA; Chattanooga *Gazette*, December 3, 1864; Cartmell Diary, January 30, 1863; Memphis *Bulletin*, June 10, 1864; Nashville *Dispatch*, December 27, 1862; *AS*, XVI, Tenn. sec., 68.

37. Oscar Handlin, *The Uprooted: The Epic Story of the Great Migrations that Made the American People* (New York, 1951), 90–91; Annette E. Church and Roberta Church, *The Robert R. Churches of Memphis: A Father and Son Who Achieved in Spite of Race* (Ann Arbor, Mich., 1974), 11–12; Davis Tillson to Clinton B. Fisk, August 21, 1865, Registered LR by the Asst. Commissioner for Ky. and

Tenn., RG 105, NA. Also see James T. Haley, *Afro-American Ency-clopedia: Thoughts, Doings, and Sayings of the Race* (Nashville, 1896), 206, 211; and J. C. Napier, "Some Negro Members of the Tennessee Legislature during Reconstruction Period and After," *Journal of Negro History,* V (January 1920), 117.

38. Edward P. Smith to M. E. Strieby, July 21, 1865, AMA; *AS,* XVIII, 44, 53; Henry H. Wright, *A History of the Sixth Iowa Infantry* (Iowa City, Iowa, 1923), 169; Mildred Throne, ed., "The Civil War Diary of C. F. Boyd, Fifteenth Iowa Infantry," *Iowa Journal of History,* L (April 1952), 175; ER-1863, 40; Powers, *Pencilings,* 112.

39. L. H. Cobb to George Whipple, December 5, 1864, AMA; First Baptist Church of Nashville Minute Book, vol. for 1860–73, 44 Dargen-Carver Library, Nashville; Daniel A. Payne, *History of the African Methodist Church,* ed. by C. S. Church (Nashville, 1891), 471–72.

40. New York *Times,* January 17, 1864; *National Freedman,* I (September 1865), 265; Powers, *Pencilings,* 67; *Freedmen's Bulletin,* I (November 1864), 45; Magdol, *Right to the Land,* 73–74; Eaton, *Grant, Lincoln, and the Freedmen,* 35.

41. Warren, ed., *Extracts from Reports,* ser. 2, 62; Caleb Perry Patterson, *The Negro in Tennessee, 1790–1865* (Austin, Tex., 1922), 152; ER-1863, 11, 17.

42. David M. Tucker, *Black Pastors and Leaders: Memphis, 1819–1972* (Memphis, 1975), 8; Fuller, *Negro Baptists,* 24; *Home Evangelist,* XV (April 1864), 15; Joseph Warren, ed., *Reports Relating to Colored Schools,* 15. Also see *Freedmen's Friend,* I (April 1865), 45; Indiana Yearly Meeting's Committee of Freedmen, *Report,* 56; ER-1863, 17; and Rose, *Rehearsal for Reconstruction,* 73–74.

43. Herbert G. Gutman, *The Black Family in Slavery and Free-dom, 1750–1925* (New York, 1978), 267–69; Augustus L. Chetlain to T. Harris, April 12, 1863, vol. 34/60–DWT, 38–39, RG 393, NA; Wills, *Army Life,* 142; *AS,* XIX, 205; Trimble, ed., "Behind the Lines," 50.

44. Joseph R. Putnam to W. D. Whipple, January 30, 1865, LR by the Department of the Cumberland, RG 393, NA; Ira Berlin, ed., *Freedom: A Documentary History of Emancipation, 1861–1867* (1 vol. to date, New York, 1982–), ser. 2, 719–20; John A. Shannon to

H. H. Deane, March 6, 1864, lst USCA (Heavy) Letterbook, 11, RG 94, NA; Augustus L. Chetlain to Lorenzo Thomas, April 5, 1864, LR by Adjutant General L. Thomas Relating to Colored Troops, RG 94, NA.

45. ER-1863, 18, 35–37.

46. Gutman, *Black Family,* chap. 1; Elizabeth Meriwether, *Recollections of 92 Years* (Nashville, 1958), 65–66; Nashville *Dispatch,* April 23, 1863; Memphis *Bulletin,* December 22, 1863.

47. Gutman, *Black Family,* 295; L. Humphrey, "Thanksgiving Day in Camp," August 20, 1863, AMA; Eaton, *Grant, Lincoln, and the Freedmen,* 34–36; John Eaton, Circular, March 19, 1864, U.S. Bureau of Refugees, Freedmen, and Abandoned Lands Circulars and Orders Collection, Memphis and Shelby County Library; L. Thomas, Order 15, March 28, 1864, L. Thomas Special Orders of Appointment Book, 105, GPB; Warren, ed., *Extracts from Reports,* ser. 1, 39. A similar order was issued by the superintendent of contrabands for the South Carolina Sea Islands. See Rose, *Rehearsal for Reconstruction,* 236.

48. ER-1864, 88; Western Freedmen's Aid Commission, *Second Annual Report,* 28; Eaton, *Grant, Lincoln, and the Freedmen,* 201–02; Warren, ed., *Extracts from Documents,* 13, 17 (quoted), 20; *Friends Review,* XVIII (February 4, 1865), 363.

49. Daniel Wadkins, "Origins and Progress before Emancipation," in G. W. Hubbard, ed., *A History of the Colored Schools of Nashville, Tennessee* (Nashville, 1874), 6; Warren, ed., *Extracts from Documents,* 5–6.

50. J. W. Wait, "The United Presbyterian Mission among the Freedmen in Nashville," and McGranahan, "Early History of Knoxville College," in McGranahan, ed., *Freedmen's Missions,* 1, 22; Levstik, ed., "Contrabands," 217; Warren, ed., *Extracts from Documents,* 7; Western Freedmen's Aid Commission, *Second Annual Report,* 33; Indiana Freedmen's Aid Commission, *Report,* 20, 24–25; Eaton, *Grant, Lincoln, and the Freedmen,* 194.

51. Joseph Warren, ed., *Report and Extracts Relating to Colored Schools* (Memphis, 1864), 7–8; *Freedmen's Friend,* I (June 1865), 60; Indiana Freedmen's Aid Commission, *Report,* 27–30; Henry S. Platt to John F. Miller, August 31, 1864, LR by the Post of Nashville, RG

393, NA; Alfred E. Anderson to W. E. Whiting, April 25, 1865, AMA. Two schools, one in Clarksville and the other in Memphis, had biracial staffs. On black teachers elsewhere in the South, see Wiley, *Southern Negroes,* 278–79; and Ripley, *Slaves and Freedmen,*138.

52. Knoxville *Whig and Rebel Ventilator,* June 11, 1864; Nashville *Dispatch,* December 10, 1863; J. W. Wait, "Mission in Nashville," in McGranahan, ed., *Freedmen's Missions,* 2–3; Indiana Freedmen's Aid Commission, *Report,* 25; Boston *Liberator,* January 29, 1864.

53. Warren, ed., *Extracts from Documents,* 8, 10; Warren, ed., *Reports Relating to Colored Schools,* 24; Rose M. Kennedy to George Whipple, May 23, 1864, AMA; ER-1864, 85–86.

54. Eaton, *Grant, Lincoln, and the Freedmen,* 4; Warren, ed., *Extracts from Documents,* 9–11. Similar school systems appeared in occupied portions of Virginia, North Carolina, and Louisiana. See Wiley, *Southern Negroes,* 262–63, 265.

55. Warren, ed., *Extracts from Documents,* 4, 14; Warren, ed., *Reports Relating to Colored Schools,* 7, 21, 24; Warren, ed., *Final Report,* 6.

56. L. Humphrey to A. S. Fiske, [1863], Alfred E. Anderson to W. E. Whiting, April 25, 1865, and E. S. Otis to George Whipple, March 1, 1864, AMA; Warren, ed., *Extracts from Reports,* ser. 1, 34; Warren, ed., *Final Report,* 6; ER-1863, 13, 25; George M. Frederickson, *The Black Image in the White Mind: The Debate on Afro-American Character and Destiny, 1817–1914* (New York, 1971), 108–09.

57. ER-1864, 82; Burton, *Diary,* 8; Western Freedmen's Aid Commission, *Appeal,* 7–8; Charles Warren, circular, May 25, 1865, U.S. Bureau of Refugees, Freedmen, and Abandoned Lands Orders and Circulars Collection, Memphis and Shelby County Library; R. D. Mussey to Andrew Johnson, February 20, 1865, Johnson Papers; L. Humphrey to A. S. Fiske, [1863], and Rose M. Kennedy to George Whipple, April 5, 1864, AMA; Indiana Freedmen's Aid Commission, *Report,* 20, 24–25.

58. Warren, ed., *Extracts from Documents,* 10 (quoted); Rose M. Kennedy to George Whipple, April 5, 1864, AMA; Indiana Freedmen's Aid Commission, *Report,* 21–24; Butchart, *Northern Schools,* 143.

59. Western Freedmen's Aid Commission, *Second Annual Report*, 33; Warren, ed., *Reports Relating to Colored Schools*, 23–24; L. Humphrey to *American Missionary* editor, June 11, 1863, and E. S. Otis to George Whipple, March 1, 1864, AMA; American Tract Society, *Freedmen's Primer* (Boston, 1864), esp. 30–41; *Freedman*, I (esp. January 1864).

60. *Freedman*, I (esp. January, April, November 1864); *AS*, XVIII, 58; Joe Barnes to S. S. Jocelyn, January 26, 1863, and L. Humphrey to A. S. Fiske, [1863], AMA.

61. Warren, ed., *Extracts from Documents*, 11. Also see R. D. Mussey to J. M. McKim, April 6, 1864, vol. 220/227–DC, 58, RG 393, NA; and Butchart, *Northern Schools*, 183.

62. Cincinnati *Gazette*, April 19, 1864 (quoted); undated McKee Diary excerpt in McGranahan, ed., *Freedmen's Missions*, 14. Nashville's public schools (for whites only) closed during the war.

63. John Lawrence to B. H. Campbell, January 26, 1865, LR by the 15th USCI, RG 94, NA; R. D. Mussey to George Mason, March 28, 1864, LR by Adjutant General L. Thomas Relating to Colored Troops, RG 94, NA; Indiana Freedmen's Aid Commission, *Report*, 27–28; Warren, ed., *Extracts from Documents*, 6.

64. *Home Evangelist*, XV (April 1864), 15; *Freedmen's Friend*, I (April 1865), 45.

Chapter 6

1. *OR*, ser. 3, III, 100–01; Dudley Taylor Cornish, *The Sable Arm: Negro Troops in the Union Army, 1861–1865* (New York, 1956), 95, 116–19, 125; *U.S. Statutes at Large*, XII, 599; Du Bois, *Black Reconstruction*, 57.

2. Fitch, *Annals*, 633; William Brunt to R. D. Mussey, May 24, 1865, Brunt's Compiled Service Record, RG 94, NA. Also see Sipes, *Seventh Pennsylvania Cavalry*, 21; and Memphis *Bulletin*, April 10, 1863.

3. Eaton, *Grant, Lincoln, and the Freedmen*, 57–58, 111; ER-1863, 19–20, 24; L. Thomas to E. D. Townsend, May 20, 1863, L. Thomas Letters and Orders Book, vol. for April–November 1863, 59–60, GPB; *OR*, ser. 1, XXIV, pt. 1, 31.

4. Bills Diary, May 18, 1863; Robert W. Cowden, *A Brief Sketch*

of the Organization and Services of the Fifty-Ninth Regiment of United States Colored Infantry (Dayton, Ohio, 1883), 39; L. Thomas to E. D. Townsend, April 7, 1863, L. Thomas Letters and Orders Book, vol. for April–November 1863, 15, GPB.

5. *OR*, ser. 3, III, 103, 560, IV, 763–65; Graf and Haskins, eds., *Johnson Papers*, VI, 489; John Hope Franklin, ed., *The Diary of James T. Ayers, Civil War Recruiter* (Springfield, Ill., 1947), xiii, 106; E. A. Paine to Andrew Johnson, July 6, 9, 13, 18, 1863, Johnson Papers; E. A. Paine to Andrew Johnson, July 20, 1863, LR by Tenn. Adjutant General, TSLA; Alvin C. Gillem to E. A. Paine, July 20, 1863, Tenn. Adjutant General Letterbook, vol. for 1863–64, 19, TSLA; Lorenzo Thomas to W. S. Rosecrans, June 15, 1863, LR by the Department of the Cumberland, RG 393, NA.

6. Frank Preston Stearns, *The Life and Public Services of George Luther Stearns* (Philadelphia, 1907), 163–64, 308 (quoted); *OR*, ser. 3, III, 684, 819–20; Nashville *Union*, September 1, 1863; James Sefton, *Andrew Johnson and the Uses of Constitutional Power* (Boston, 1980), 70.

7. *OR*, ser. 3, III, 816–17, 820, 823 (quoted), 837, 840, 855–56, 861; Nashville *Union*, December 5, 1863.

8. Augustus L. Chetlain, *Recollections of Seventy Years* (Galena, Ill., 1899), 100; *OR*, ser. 3, IV, 90, 765–66; Stearns, *Stearns*, 322–23.

9. Chetlain, *Recollections*, 46, 67; *Williams' Cincinnati Directory* (Cincinnati, 1860), 231; R. D. Mussey to Mr. Meyer, March 27, 1864, vol. 220/227–DC, 35, RG 393, NA.

10. *AS*, XVIII, 218 (quoted); Stearns, *Stearns*, 317; Charles R. Thompson to J. A. Garfield, August 25, 1863, 12th USCI Letterbook, 2, RG 94, NA; R. D. Mussey to George Mason, April 11, 1864, and R. D. Mussey to C. P. Brown, November 7, 1864, LR by Adjutant General L. Thomas Relating to Colored Troops, RG 94, NA; Litwack, *Been in the Storm*, 75–79.

11. J. H. Cochran to W. T. Spurgin, August 9, 1864, vol. 221–DC, 7, RG 393, NA; *Senate Executive Documents*, 38 Cong., 2 Sess., No. 28, 10–11; John Phillips, circular, April 4, 1864, LR by the 59th USCI, RG 94, NA; Nashville *Press*, November 27, 1863.

12. ER-1864, 19; Nashville *Press*, April 21, 1864; Cowden, *Brief Sketch*, 38–39; *U.S. Statutes at Large*, XIII, 144, 379.

13. William F. Wheeler to George L. Stearns, October 22, 1863, and James N. Holmes to George L. Stearns, October 8, 1863, Records of Maj. George L. Stearns, RG 393, NA; William B. Gaw to R. D. Mussey, January 24, 1864, 16th USCI Letterbook (unpaginated), RG 94, NA; Stearns, *Stearns*, 313; R. D. Mussey to George B. Halstead, May 30, 1864, LR by Adjutant General L. Thomas Relating to Colored Troops, RG 94, NA; *AS*, XVIII, 218 (quoted). On the use of black recruiting patrols elsewhere, see Charles Lewis Wagandt, *The Mighty Revolution: Negro Emancipation in Maryland, 1862–1864* (Baltimore, 1964), 199.

14. Boston *Liberator*, January 29, 1864; Chicago *Tribune*, October 9, 1863 (quoted).

15. Cartmell Diary, June 1, 1863; Bills Diary, July 22, 1863; *OR*, ser. 3, III, 686–87; U. S. Grant, G.O. 53, August 23, 1863, vol. 13/21–DT, 224–25, RG 393, NA; *U.S. Statutes at Large*, XII, 731–37. On the conscription of blacks elsewhere, see Rose, *Rehearsal for Reconstruction*, 145; Ripley, *Slaves and Freedmen*, 107–08; Howard, *Black Liberation*, 65; and Wagandt, *Mighty Revolution*, 198.

16. Knoxville *Whig and Rebel Ventilator*, January 16, 1864; J. D. Webster to G. A. Williams, January 29, 1864, LR by the District of Memphis, RG 393, NA; R. P. Buckland endorsement on I. G. Kappner to G. W. Dustan, January 26, 1864, LR by Fort Pickering, RG 393, NA; Augustus L. Chetlain, S.O. 27, May 6, 1864, vol. 36/66A–DWT (unpaginated), RG 393, NA.

17. ER-1864, 78–79; Augustus L. Chetlain, circular, April 12, 1864, vol. 34/60–DWT, 40, RG 393, NA; Augustus L. Chetlain, G.O. 18, June 23, 1864, vol. 36/66–DWT (unpaginated), RG 393, NA; George L. Paddock to Charles P. Brown, July 21, 1864, LR by the 17th USCI, RG 94, NA; Chattanooga *Gazette*, November 23, 1864.

18. George L. Stearns testimony, 66, AFIC; Henry R. Mizner to ?, December 15, 1863, LR by the 15th USCI, RG 94, NA; Porter Diary, January 19, 1864; W. R. Shafter to R. D. Mussey, January 30, 1864, LR by the District of Middle Tennessee, RG 393, NA; *Senate Executive Documents*, 38 Cong., 2 Sess., No. 28, 2.

19. Trimble, ed., "Behind the Lines," 71; William Gaw to R. D. Mussey, February 17, 1864, LR by the 15th USCI, RG 94, NA;

T. Jefferson Downey to R. D. Mussey, February 24, 1864, Records of
Capt. R. D. Mussey, RG 393, NA.

20. Simon, ed., *Grant Papers*, X, 107, 178 (quoted); L. H. Rousseau, G.O. 10, March 7, 1864, vol. 9–DMT, 26, RG 393, NA.

21. R. D. Mussey to Lt. Osborn, April 6, 1864, R. D. Mussey to
Byron O. Camp, May 13, 1864, and R. D. Mussey to D. K. Carter,
June 26, 1864, vol. 220/227–DC, 56, 102, 170, RG 393, NA; R. D.
Mussey, memorandum, August 18, 1864, vol. 221–DC, 50–51, RG
393, NA; Howard, *Black Liberation*, 66, 74; Nashville *Times and True
Union*, October 1, 1864; Chattanooga *Gazette*, December 17, 20,
1864; Memphis *Bulletin*, January 20, 1865; Edward S. Richards to
Andrew Johnson, January 10, 1865, Johnson Papers.

22. B. H. Polk to R. D. Mussey, December 11, 1863, vol. 2–DMT,
36, RG 393, NA; John A. Shannon to H. H. Deane, May 27, 1864, 1st
USCA (Heavy) Letterbook, 26–27, RG 94, NA; J. R. Putnam to R. D.
Mussey, July 18, 1864, 42nd USCI Letterbook (unpaginated), RG 94,
NA.

23. Henry Romeyn, *With Colored Troops in the Army of the Cumberland* (n.p., 1904), 8; *OR*, ser. 1, XXI, pt. 3, 366–67, ser. 3, IV,
433–34; William T. Sherman to Lorenzo Thomas, June 21, 26, 1864,
Sherman Letterbook I (incorrectly marked F on the cover), 231, 245–
46, GPB; R. D. Mussey to George B. Halstead, June 8, 25, 1864, LR
by Adjutant General L. Thomas Relating to Colored Troops, RG 94,
NA; W. D. Whipple to R. D. Mussey, June 19, 30, 1864, vol.
223/431–DC, 128–29, RG 393, NA. Franklin, ed., *Ayers Diary*, xviii,
claims that Sherman soon revoked his order, but this author found no
evidence to that effect.

24. *U.S. Statutes at Large*, XIII, 379; R. D. Mussey to Charles
Foster, August 8, 1864, vol. 221–DC, 1, RG 393, NA; James O. Pierce
to N. J. T. Dana, February 11, 1865, vol. 5–DMiss (unpaginated), RG
393, NA.

25. R. D. Mussey to J. M. McKim, August 14, 1864 (quoted),
R. D. Mussey to C. P. Lyman, September 3, 1864, and R. D. Mussey
to J. D. Webster, October 1, 1864, vol. 221–DC, 31, 96, 188, RG 393,
NA; George H. Thomas, Court Martial Order 2, January 24, 1865,
Department of the Cumberland Printed Orders, RG 393, NA;
L. Thomas to E. D. Townsend, July 22, 1864, L. Thomas Letterbook,

vol. for July 1864–June 1865, 26–27, GPB; *U.S. Statutes at Large,* XIII, 491.

26. *OR,* ser. 3, III, 44, V, 13, 662; *U.S. Statutes at Large,* XIII, 44. The percentage of males of military age who joined the federal army from all Confederate states was 14 percent for blacks and 8 percent for whites.

27. Cowden, *Brief Sketch,* 45–46; Henry V. Freeman, "A Colored Brigade in the Campaign and Battle of Nashville," in Military Order of the Loyal Legion of the U.S., Illinois Commandery, *Military Essays and Recollections* (2 vols., Chicago, 1896), II, 400; Thomas J. Morgan, *Reminiscences of Service with Colored Troops in the Army of the Cumberland, 1863–65* (Providence, R. I., 1885), 20, 24 (quoted).

28. Augustus L. Chetlain, G.O. 14, May 14, 1864, vol. 36/66–DWT, 23, RG 393, NA; J. A. Copeland to J. P. Harper, November 19, 1864, vol. 27/42–DWT, 227–28, RG 393, NA; R. D. Mussey to Charles Foster, [June 1864], vol. 220/227–DC, 175, RG 393, NA; Charles W. Bennett and John M. Woodruff to John A. Hottenstein, December 12, 1864, LR by the 13th USCI, RG 94, NA; Nashville *Union,* March 10, 1864 (quoted).

29. David Donald, "Died of Democracy," in David Donald, ed., *Why the North Won the Civil War* (Baton Rouge, La., 1960), 82; Genovese, *Roll, Jordan, Roll,* 149.

30. Endorsement by Thomas Trauernich on F. O. Bynes to George L. Stearns, October 2, 1863, Records of Maj. George L. Stearns, RG 393, NA; *AS,* XVIII, 258; John Foley to T. Harris, January 11, 1865, Unregistered LR by the District of West Tennessee, RG 393, NA; Henry McLean to L. Methundy, November 3, 1863, LR by Fort Pickering, RG 393, NA; Charles W. Bennett and John M. Woodruff to John A. Hottenstein, December 12, 1864, LR by the 13th USCI, RG 94, NA; Berlin, ed., *Freedom,* ser. 2, 462.

31. Robert Cowden to Lorenzo Thomas, December 1, 1864, and Robert Cowden to W. W. Deane, August 29, 1865, LR by the 59th USCI, RG 94, NA; J. R. Putnam to Lorenzo Thomas, August 2, 1865, 42nd USCI Letterbook (unpaginated), RG 94, NA; L. Johnson to Lorenzo Thomas, December 18, 1865, 44th USCI Letterbook, 57, RG 94, NA.

32. *Freedmen's Bulletin*, I (March 1865), 79; Cowden, *Brief Sketch*, 61; *OR*, ser. 3, IV, 771; Morgan, *Reminiscences*, 23; Cincinnati *Gazette*, March 14, 1864; Western Freedmen's Aid Commission, *Appeal*, 7.

33. Indiana Freedmen's Aid Commission, *Report*, 26; C. P. Taylor to Lorenzo Thomas, May 1, 1865, LR by the 3rd USCA (Heavy), RG 94, NA; Romeyn, *With Colored Troops*, 10.

34. *AS*, XIX, 179–80; William B. Gaw to R. D. Mussey, January 2, 1864 (quoted), 16th USCI Letterbook (unpaginated), RG 94, NA. Also see Morgan, *Reminiscences*, 16–17; and Freeman, "Colored Brigade," 400.

35. Edmondson Diary, May 4, 1864; Cartmell Diary, February 2, 1863; Memphis *Bulletin*, February 20, 1864; Nashville *Press*, April 19, 1864; Cowden, *Brief Sketch*, 53–54.

36. McDowell, *Fiddles*, 232; John O'Flanagan to Andrew Johnson, August 7, 1864, Johnson Papers; Austin O. Lyn to ?, August 14, 1865, vol. 2–DET, 244, RG 393, NA; C. H. Thompson to W. W. Deane, February 15, 1865, LR by the 1st USCA (Heavy), RG 94, NA; Jane Washington to George A. Washington, July 25, 1864, Washington Papers.

37. Cincinnati *Gazette*, October 28, 1863 (quoted); R. D. Mussey to George Mason, March 14, April 4, 1864, and R. D. Mussey to C. P. Brown, August 8, 1864, LR by Adjutant General L. Thomas Relating to Colored Troops, RG 94, NA; Nashville *Union*, May 3, 1864; Nashville *Times and True Union*, September 27, 1864; Morgan, *Reminiscences*, 20.

38. Paul E. Reiger, ed., *Through One Man's Eyes: The Civil War Experiences of a Belmont County Volunteer* (Mount Vernon, Ohio, 1974), 63. Also see Knoxville *Whig and Rebel Ventilator*, January 16, 1864; and Nashville *Union*, August 25, 1864.

39. Wiley, *Billy Yank*, 120–21; Du Bois, *Black Reconstruction*, 104, 110; McGee, *72d Indiana Infantry*, 227 (quoted).

40. M. T. Williamson to B. K. Roberts, February 1, 1865, LR by the District of West Tennessee, RG 393, NA; Augustus L. Chetlain to Lorenzo Thomas, May 10, 1864, vol. 34/60–DWT, 58, RG 393, NA.

41. H. H. Hood to R. J. Irwin, September 9, 1863, and all of its endorsements, LR by the 3rd USCA (Heavy), RG 94, NA; New York

Anglo-African, August 19, 1865; Lorenzo Thomas to George H. Thomas, June 27, 1864, L. Thomas Letters and Orders Book, vol. for November 1863–July 1864, 137, GPB; William D. Whipple to J. L. Donelson, June 28, 1864, LR by the Post of Nashville, RG 393, NA.

42. *U.S. Statutes at Large*, XII, 599; *OR*, ser. 3, III, 420, 816; Cornish, *Sable Arm*, 187–88, 192–95; I. G. Kappner to Henry Binmore, September 2, 1863, 3rd USCA (Heavy) Letterbook, 19, RG 94, NA; Romeyn, *With Colored Troops*, 12; *U.S. Statutes at Large*, XIII, 129.

43. Tennessee Civil War Centennial Commission, *Tennesseans in the Civil War*, I, 405, 410; Eaton, *Grant, Lincoln, and the Freedmen*, 107–09; T. Jefferson Downey to James F. Rusling, May 18, 1864, 15th USCI Letterbook, 3, RG 94, NA; J. P. Harper to Lorenzo Thomas, November 7, 1864, LR by the 3rd USCA (Heavy), RG 94, NA.

44. Berlin, ed., *Freedom*, ser. 2, 489, 501; ER-1864, 78–80; R. D. Mussey to George Mason, April 11, 1864, LR by Adjutant General L. Thomas Relating to Colored Troops, RG 94, NA; William T. Sherman to Lorenzo Thomas, July 25, 1864, Sherman Letterbook J, 124, GPB; Morgan, *Reminiscences*, 22, 25; *AS*, supp. ser. 2, III, 818 (quoted).

45. *OR*, ser. 1, XXXI, pt. 1, 583–85. For more detailed descriptions of the major Tennessee battles involving black troops, see Albert Castel, "The Fort Pillow Massacre: A Fresh Examination of the Evidence," *Civil War History*, IV (March 1958), 37–50; and Bobby L. Lovett, "The Negro's Civil War in Tennessee, 1861–1865," *Journal of Negro History*, LXI (January 1976), 47–48.

46. *OR*, ser. 2, V, 797, 844, 940–41.

47. Cornish, *Sable Arm*, 240–42, 259, 267; Robert Selph Henry, *"First with the Most" Forrest* (New York 1944), 245, 250. Ronald K. Huch, "Fort Pillow Massacre: The Aftermath of Paducah," *Illinois State Historical Society Journal*, LXVI (Spring 1973), 65, 70, incorrectly assumes that Forrest used the same troops in both battles.

48. *OR*, ser. 1, XXXII, pt. 1, 520, 560–61, 609; John Cimprich and Robert C. Mainfort, eds., "Fort Pillow Revisited: New Evidence about an Old Controversy," *Civil War History*, XXVIII (December 1982), 299–300, 301 (quoted); George Bodnia, ed., "Fort Pillow Massacre: Observations of a Minnesotan," *Minnesota History*, XLIII (Spring 1973), 188.

49. Thomas Jordan and J. P. Pryor, *The Campaigns of Lieutenant General N. B. Forrest* (New York, 1868), 439; John Allen Wyeth, *Life of General Nathan Bedford Forrest* (New York, 1899), 355–56; J. Harvey Mathes, *General Forrest* (New York, 1902), 227; Eric W. Sheppard, *Bedford Forrest: The Confederacy's Greatest Cavalryman* (New York, 1930), 170–72; Andrew N. Lytle, *Bedford Forrest and His Critter Company* (New York, 1931), 279; Henry, *Forrest*, 256–66; John L. Jordan, "Was There a Massacre at Fort Pillow?" *Tennessee Historical Quarterly*, VI (June 1947), 120–32; Atlanta *Memphis Appeal*, May 13, 1864.

50. *OR*, ser. 1, XXXII, pt. 1, 539, 561–66, 610, pt. 3, 822; Cimprich and Mainfort, eds., "Fort Pillow," 303.

51. Cimprich and Mainfort, eds., "Fort Pillow," 299–300.

52. Compiled Service Records of the 11th USCI, 2nd USCA (Light), Bradford Battalion, 6th Tenn. Cavalry, 14th Tenn. Cavalry, Thomas C. George, John T. Young, and Alvaro J. W. Thompson, RG 94, NA; Monthly Return for March 1864, Muster Rolls of the Bradford Battalion, RG 94, NA; Mound City and Memphis Hospital Registers, April 1864, RG 94, NA; Silver Cloud parolee list, April 13, 1864, Letters from Squadron Officers, RG 24, NA; John Cimprich and Robert C. Mainfort, "Statistical Analysis of the Fort Pillow Massacre" (unpublished paper in the author's possession).

53. Cimprich and Mainfort, eds., "Fort Pillow," 304.

54. Cairo (Ill.) *News* excerpt in Chicago *Tribune*, April 18, 1864; *OR*, ser. 1, XXXII, pt. 1, 525, 532, 535–36, 563, 597; *Senate Committee Reports*, 38 Cong., 1 Sess., No. 63, 22; Cimprich and Mainfort, eds., "Fort Pillow," 299–300 (quoted).

55. *OR*, ser. 1, XXXII, pt. 1, 558, 610.

56. Ibid., 590; Memphis *Bulletin*, April 28, 1864; Cornish, *Sable Arm*, 176–77; *Senate Committee Reports*, 38 Cong., 1 Sess., No. 63, passim.

57. Morgan, *Reminiscences*, 31–32; Romeyn, *With Colored Troops*, 18–21; R. D. Mussey to C. P. Brown, December 5, 1864, LR by Adjutant General L. Thomas Relating to Colored Troops, RG 94, NA.

58. Cornish, *Sable Arm*, 283; *OR*, ser. 1, XLV, pt. 1, 504–05.

59. *OR*, ser. 1, XLV, pt. 1, 505; Freeman, "Colored Brigade," 413–

15; George H. Thomas Journal, December 15–16, 1864, GPB; Morgan, *Reminiscences*, 48–49 (quoted).

Chapter 7

1. *Congressional Globe*, 37 Cong., 1 Sess., 223 (July 22, 1861), 257, 265 (July 25, 1861).

2. Cincinnati *Gazette*, March 20, 29, April 5, 1862; Memphis *Bulletin*, July 13, September 9, 1862; Chicago *Tribune*, May 21, 1862; Nashville *Union*, April 26, July 6, 1862; New York *National Antislavery Standard*, April 5, 1862. Hall, *Johnson*, 91–92, 106, and Sefton, *Johnson*, 93–94, incorrectly contend that Johnson's early rhetorical threats constituted a full endorsement of emancipation.

3. New York *Times*, September 9, 1862; Memphis *Bulletin*, July 29, 1862; Nashville *Union*, May 23, 30, June 27, 1862.

4. *Congressional Globe*, 37 Cong., 2 Sess., 959 (February 25, 1862), 3267–68 (July 11, 1862), Appendix, 191 (May 24, 1862), 273–74 (May 23, 1862).

5. Ibid., 37 Cong., 2 Sess., 2533–34 (June 3, 1862), Appendix, 191–92 (May 24, 1862); Nashville *Union*, July 26, 1862.

6. C. W. Charlton to T. A. R. Nelson, October 5, 1862, and Samuel Jones to T. A. R. Nelson, October 17, 1862, Nelson Papers; Athens *Post*, October 10, 1862; Knoxville *Register*, October 5, 1862 (quoted); Palmer, *Recollections*, 127; Cincinnati *Gazette*, November 17, 1862; Memphis *Bulletin*, November 9, 1862.

7. *U.S. Statutes at Large*, XII, 1267; *OR*, ser. 3, II, 675 (quoted); Patton, *Unionism*, 28–29.

8. Maslowski, *Treason Must Be Made Odious*, 78–79; Graf and Haskins, eds., *Johnson Papers*, VI, 44, 50, 78, 92; *House Committee Reports*, 37 Cong., 3 Sess., No. 46, 8.

9. Nashville *Press and Times*, July 6, 1865; Graf and Haskins, eds., *Johnson Papers*, VI, 85–86; William G. Brownlow to Abraham Lincoln, December 25, 1862, Lincoln Papers; Memphis *Bulletin*, October 6, 1863; Cincinnati *Gazette*, December 24, 1862.

10. Memphis *Bulletin*, November 28, December 27, 1862; Graf and Haskins, eds., *Johnson Papers*, VI, 102; *House Committee Re-*

ports, 37 Cong., 3 Sess., No. 46, 3, 8; *U.S. Statutes at Large*, XII, 1269.

11. Ripley, *Slaves and Freedmen*, 162–63; Richard Orr Curry, *A House Divided: A Study of Statehood Politics and the Copperhead Movement in West Virginia* (Pittsburgh, 1964), 10–11; Nashville *Union*, April 23, June 13, 1863; Cincinnati *Gazette*, April 17, 1863; Nashville *Press*, May 16, 1863; Graf and Haskins, eds., *Johnson Papers*, VI, 156, 337; Horace Maynard, *To the Slaveholders of Tennessee* (n.p., 1863), 21–23.

12. Nashville *Dispatch*, July 7, 1863; Memphis *Argus*, September 4, 1863; Nashville *Union*, October 1, 4, 1863.

13. *OR*, ser. 3, III, 103, 123.

14. Sefton, *Johnson*, 22, 41, 45; Graf and Haskins, eds., *Johnson Papers*, VI, 344 (quoted).

15. *OR*, ser. 1, XXX, pt. 1, 182–83; Tennessee Constitution (1834), art. II, sec. 31, art. XI, sec. 3; Graf and Haskins, eds., *Johnson Papers*, VI, 490.

16. Stearns, *Stearns*, 309–10; Graf and Haskins, eds., *Johnson Papers*, VI, 363, 377–78.

17. George L. Stearns to Charles Sumner, October 9, 1863, Charles Sumner Papers, Houghton Library, Harvard University, Cambridge, Mass.; Loyal Citizens of Tennessee Petition, October 10, 1863, Lincoln Papers; Nashville *Dispatch*, January 1, 2, 9, 16, 1864.

18. Philadelphia *Press*, July 18, 1863; Boston *Liberator*, January 29, 1864 (quoted).

19. Nashville *Union*, January 1, 1864; Nashville *Dispatch*, August 16, 1864; Nashville *Times and True Union*, July 6, October 24, 25, 1864; Memphis *Bulletin*, June 7, August 2, 1864, January 3, 1865.

20. Graf and Haskins, eds., *Johnson Papers*, VI, 557; Hall, *Johnson*, 114, 118; Nashville *Press*, January 22, 1864; Tennessee Constitution (1834), art. 1, sec. 1.

21. Memphis *Bulletin*, October 6, 1863, January 27, March 5, 1864; Hall, *Johnson*, 119; Porter Diary, June 5, 1864.

22. Knoxville *Whig and Rebel Ventilator*, February 6, April 16, 1864; New York *Times*, February 22, 1864; Nashville *Union*, February 7, 1864; Nashville *Times and True Union*, March 14, 1864; Cincinnati *Gazette*, February 27, 1864; William E. Parrish, *Missouri under*

Radical Rule, 1865–1870 (Columbia, Mo., 1965), 3–4; Curry, *House Divided*, 103–04, 128–29; Graf and Haskins, eds., *Johnson Papers*, VI, 349 (quoted), 675.

23. William B. Carter to William B. Campbell, September 28, 1864, Campbell Papers; Nashville *Times and True Union*, April 23, 1864; Cincinnati *Gazette*, April 22, 1864; Temple, *Notable Men*, 407–08; New York *Tribune*, April 30, 1864.

24. Nashville *Union*, April 13, 1864; Nashville *Times and True Union*, October 1, 25, 1864; Knoxville *Whig and Rebel Ventilator*, November 11, 23, 1863; Memphis *Bulletin*, May 24, 1864.

25. Hinton R. Helper, *The Impending Crisis of the South: How to Meet It* (New York, 1857), passim; Knoxville *Whig and Rebel Ventilator*, May 7, 1864; Maynard, *To the Slaveholders*, 16, 22; Memphis *Bulletin*, March 5, 1864; Chattanooga *Gazette*, March 5 (quoted), July 18, 1864.

26. Knoxville *Whig and Rebel Ventilator*, November 1, 1863; [Gilmore], *Down in Tennessee*, 220; Philadelphia *Enquirer*, December 2, 1863; Nashville *Times and True Union*, April 15, September 10, 1864; Nashville *Union*, June 4 (quoted), 28, 1864.

27. R. F. Stevens to William B. Campbell, November 12, 1863, and William B. Carter to William B. Campbell, September 28, 1864, Campbell Papers; Chicago *Tribune*, August 28, September 28, 1864.

28. Nashville *Times and True Union*, April 16, 1864; Nashville *Press*, February 2, July 7, 1864 (quoted).

29. Cincinnati *Gazette*, April 22, 1864; William B. Carter to William B. Campbell, September 28, 1864 (quoted), Campbell Papers; Nashville *Press*, January 12 (quoted), 29, 1864; J. Netherland to Andrew Johnson, July 8, 1864, Johnson Papers; Nashville *Dispatch*, October 20, 1864.

30. Nashville *Times and True Union*, September 8, 1864; Memphis *Bulletin*, September 14, 1864.

31. Edward S. Richards to H. Brooks, July 9, 1864, Tenn. Adjutant General Letterbook, vol. for 1864–65, 24, TSLA; Nashville *Press*, July 9, 1864; Nashville *Times and True Union*, July 11, October 2, 1864; George H. Thomas, G.O. 45, October 17, 1864 (quoted), Department of the Cumberland Printed Orders for 1863–64, RG 393, NA; Hall, *Johnson*, 147–53.

32. John Hambright to J. Hambright, June 17, 1864, and J. B. Bingham to Andrew Johnson, November 9, 1864, Johnson Papers; Graf and Haskins, eds., *Johnson Papers,* VI, 663; Knoxville *Whig and Rebel Ventilator,* June 11, 1864; Nashville *Times and True Union,* August 25, September 15, 1864; Memphis *Bulletin,* July 6, 1864; Chattanooga *Gazette,* June 1, 1864; Reiger, ed., *Through One Man's Eyes,* 93 (quoted). Congress refused to count Tennessee's electoral votes on the grounds that insurrection had not entirely ended in the state.

33. Thomas B. Alexander, *Political Reconstruction in Tennessee* (Nashville, 1950), 129; Hughes, *Thirty Years,* 13, 111–12; Schweninger, "Free-Slave Phenomenon," 301–02.

34. Memphis *Bulletin,* January 3, 1865; Boston *Liberator,* January 29, 1864; Nashville *Times and True Union,* September 27, October 24, 1864, January 4, 20, February 25, 1865; Nashville *Dispatch,* August 16, 1864; Nashville *Union,* January 1, 1864; Philadelphia *Christian Recorder,* August 26, 1865; Nashville *Colored Tennessean,* August 12, 1865; Nashville *Press and Times,* May 29, 1865. Information on black leaders happens to be more available for Nashville than for the other cities.

35. 1860 Census Population Schedule for Davidson, Knox, and Shelby counties, RG 29, NA; Nashville *Press and Times,* April 4, 1868; Napier, "Negro Members," 117; P. L. Nichol to Andrew Johnson, October 21, 1864, Johnson Papers; Norton, *Tennessee Christians,* 130; Tucker, *Black Pastors,* 7–8; New York *Anglo-African,* August 12, 1865; New York *National Antislavery Standard,* October 17, 1863; Schweninger, "Free-Slave Phenomenon," 302. More than half of the leaders could not be identified.

36. Taylor, *Negro in Tennessee,* 53, 163, 232, 246, 251.

37. Nashville *Times and True Union,* August 16, 1864, January 4, 1865; National Convention of Colored Men, *Proceedings* (Boston, 1864), passim. On the black suffrage movement in other occupied areas, see Ripley, *Slaves and Freedmen,* 164, 173–80; and Rose, *Rehearsal for Reconstruction,* 316–17.

38. Louisville *Journal,* August 3, 1864; Porter Diary, October 29, 1864; Nashville *Times and True Union,* October 25, November 9, 1864; Nashville *Press,* October 26, 1864.

39. R. D. Mussey to George L. Stearns, August 17, 1864, vol. 221–DC, 44–46, RG 393, NA; *Freedmen's Bulletin*, I (July 1865), 136 (quoted).

40. Philadelphia *Enquirer*, December 2, 1863; Western Freedmen's Aid Commission, *Second Annual Report*, 40–41; Nashville *Times and True Union*, April 26, October 25, November 14, 1864; Memphis *Bulletin*, January 3, 1865; Nashville *Press*, October 26, 1864; "Jeff Davis" to Andrew Johnson, October 24, 1864, Johnson Papers.

41. Nashville *Dispatch*, October 15, 20, 1864; [Gilmore], *Down in Tennessee*, 220–21; Chattanooga *Gazette*, June 19, 1864; Temple, *Notable Men*, 408; Knoxville *Whig and Rebel Ventilator*, April 23, 1864 (quoted).

42. Nashville *Times and True Union*, October 25, November 14, 1864.

43. This characterization of Johnson qualifies and builds upon interpretations in Kenneth M. Stampp, *The Era of Reconstruction, 1865–1877* (New York, 1965), 54–82; John H. Cox and LaWanda Cox, *Politics, Principle, and Prejudice, 1865–1866: Dilemma of Reconstruction America* (New York, 1963), 95–105; and Michael Les Benedict, *The Impeachment and Trial of Andrew Johnson* (New York, 1973), 3–7.

44. Knoxville *Whig and Rebel Ventilator*, November 16, 1864; Nashville *Times and True Union*, November 5, 28, 1864 (quoted).

45. Nashville *Times and True Union*, January 10–14, 1865.

46. Ibid., January 12, 14, 16, 18 (quoted), 20, 1865; Chicago *Tribune*, January 18, 1865; New York *Tribune*, January 24, 1865; Nashville *Press*, January 13, 1865; Nashville *Dispatch*, January 13, 1865. The Louisiana constitutional convention of 1864 had resolved the black suffrage issue in the same way. See Ripley, *Slaves and Freedmen*, 171–73.

47. Nashville *Union*, January 25, 27, February 7, 11, 1865; P. E. Bland et al. to Andrew Johnson, February 3, 1865, Johnson Papers; *U.S. Statutes at Large*, XIII, 738; Memphis *Bulletin*, February 21, 1865; Nashville *Dispatch*, February 21, 1865.

48. Alexander, *Reconstruction in Tennessee*, 33; Nashville *Union*, February 4, 1865; Nashville *Press*, February 15, 1865; Nashville *Dis-*

patch, February 21, 1865; Nashville *Times and True Union,* February 25, 1865; Tally Sheets of Elections, 1860–69, TSLA. Unionist state governments preceding Tennessee were Arkansas (January 1864), Virginia (April 1864), Louisiana (September 1864), Maryland (October 1864), and Missouri (January 1865).

Chapter 8

1. Cincinnati *Gazette,* April 6, 1865; Tennessee, *Senate Journal,* 1865–67 General Assembly, 1 Sess., 15 (April 5, 1865). For developments similar to those treated in this chapter but occurring elsewhere, see E. Merton Coulter, "Slavery and Freedom in Athens, Georgia, 1860–66," *Georgia Historical Quarterly,* XLIX (September 1965), 285–90; Escott, *Slavery Remembered,* 132–42; Litwack, *Been in the Storm,* chaps. 4–5; Ripley, *Slaves and Freedmen,* chap. 10; Williamson, *After Slavery,* chaps. 2–4; M. G. Smith, "Slavery and Emancipation in Two Societies," *Social and Economic Studies,* III (December 1954), 275–84; and Robert Brent Toplin, *The Abolition of Slavery in Brazil* (New York, 1972), 259–62.

2. Mary Wilkin, ed., "Some Papers of the American Cotton Planters' Association, 1865–1866," *Tennessee Historical Quarterly,* VII (December 1948), 343; R. J. Hinton to Clinton B. Fisk, September 8, 1865, Registered LR by the Asst. Commissioner for Ky. and Tenn., RG 105, NA; Meriwether, *Recollections,* 181; Hampton J. Cheney file, Confederate Veterans Questionnaires, TSLA; A. J. Fletcher to Jehu Baker, December 29, 1865, William G. Brownlow/Jehu Baker Correspondence, TSLA; Clinton B. Fisk to Oliver O. Howard, July 6, 1865, Tenn. vol. 15, 18, RG 105, NA.

3. Nashville *Press and Times,* July 6, 13, 1865; Cincinnati *Gazette,* June 24, 1865; Nashville *Union,* November 14, 1865 (quoted).

4. Nashville *Press and Times,* July 14, 1865 (quoted); A. J. Fletcher to Andrew Johnson, July 20, 1865, Johnson Papers; Andrew Johnson to George H. Thomas, July 21, 1865, Pressbook, 160, Johnson Papers; Nashville *Union,* November 14, 1865; Nashville *Dispatch,* July 23 (quoted), November 23, 1865.

5. *AS,* XI, pt. 7, 193, XVIII, 267, 306; Nashville *Press and Times,* July 11, 1865; Chicago *Tribune,* September 24, 1865; J. T.

Trowbridge, *The South: A Tour of Its Battlefields and Ruined Cities* (Hartford, Conn., 1866), 341; R. D. Mussey to Southard Hoffman, March 17, 1865, Tenn. vol. 8, 23, RG 105, NA; Dabney Affidavit, August 12, 1865, LR by the La Grange Superintendent, RG 105, NA; T. A. Walker to W. W. Deane, July 19, 1865, Unregistered LR by the Memphis Subassistant Commissioner, RG 105, NA.

6. Joe Black affidavit, July 18, 1865 (quoted), Unregistered LR by the Memphis Subassistant Commissioner, RG 105, NA; M. H. Puckett to Clinton B. Fisk, January 15, 1866, Reports of Outrages filed with the Asst. Commissioner for Ky. and Tenn., RG 105, NA; J. D. Stillman to Davis Tillson, June 21, 1865, Tenn. vol. 128, 1, 4, RG 105, NA; New York *Tribune*, October 8, 1865; Isaac Thompson to Davis Tillson, August 15, 1865, Unregistered LR by the Memphis Subassistant Commissioner, RG 105, NA.

7. John W. Jones to N. A. M. Dudley, December 8, 1865, Unregistered LR by the Memphis Subassistant Commissioner, RG 105, NA; Clinton B. Fisk to Oliver O. Howard, July 6, 1865, Tenn. vol. 15, 18, RG 105, NA; Memphis *Argus,* May 30, 1865.

8. *AS*, supp. ser. 2, VIII, 3027; M. H. Puckett to Clinton B. Fisk, January 15, 1866, Reports of Outrages filed with the Asst. Commissioner for Ky. and Tenn., RG 105, NA; Davis Tillson to W. T. Clarke, July 21, 1865, Registered LR by the Asst. Commissioner for Ky. and Tenn., RG 105, NA.

9. *AS*, XVI, Tenn. sec., 1, 21, XVIII, 62, 183; Nashville *Union,* May 6, 1865; Cincinnati *Gazette,* August 19, 1865; N. A. M. Dudley to ?, July 21, 1865, vol. 58/64–DMT, 52, RG 393, NA. Unlike some other states, Tennessee did not encounter a large-scale problem in the apprenticing of black children without parental consent in 1865. See Gutman, *Black Family,* 402–12.

10. John S. Claybrooke to a brother, [July 1865], Tenn. Secretary of State Papers, TSLA; *AS*, VIII, pt. 2, 128.

11. Margaret [?] to a sister, March 5, 1865, Campbell Papers; *AS*, XI, pt. 7, 147; Armstrong, *Old Massa's People,* 320–21.

12. *AS*, XVIII, 250 (quoted); R. J. Hinton to W. T. Clarke, September 18, 1865, Registered LR by the Asst. Commissioner for Ky. and Tenn., RG 105, NA.

13. *AS*, supp. ser. 2, III, 876–77, VI, 2285.

14. *AS*, XVIII, 134–35, 138; Meriwether, *Recollections*, 172–73 (quoted); Emily Donelson Walton, *Autobiography* (n.p., 1932), 41; Julia Morgan, *How It Was: Four Years among the Rebels* (Nashville, 1892), 163; Litwack, *Been in the Storm*, 216. Also see Barker Diary, January 10, 1866.

15. [C. W. Hall], *Threescore Years and Ten* (Cincinnati, 1884), 227; Memphis *Bulletin*, May 2, 31, 1865; Cartmell Diary, August 7, 1865. Also see Porter Diary, February 22, 1865, Isaac Lane Interview, September 5, 1932, Wiley Papers; and *AS*, XVIII, 161, supp. ser. 2, IX, 3452, 3845.

16. Nashville *Union*, November 14, 1865; Thomas H. Coldwell, *Reports of Cases Argued and Determined in the Supreme Court of Tennessee* (7 vols., Nashville, 1901), II, 13; Memphis *Argus*, August 20, October 24, 1865; Columbia *Herald* excerpt in Nashville *Dispatch*, September 13, 1865; Clarksville *Chronicle*, October 6, 1865; Nashville *Union*, September 20, December 19, 1865.

17. Talcott Parsons, *The Social System* (New York, 1951), 491.

18. Tennessee, *Senate Journal Appendix*, 35th General Assembly, 1 Sess., 74–76; Tennessee Proceedings, 7, 31, and Tennessee Register, passim, Records of the Slave Claims Commission, RG 94, NA; Alexander, *Reconstruction in Tennessee*, 50.

19. Alexander, *Reconstruction in Tennessee*, 50–51; New York *Anglo-African*, December 16, 1865; Bureau Court Cases in Memphis, Tenn. vols. 169–70, passim, RG 105, NA; Clarksville *Chronicle*, September 1, 1865 (quoted).

20. Litwack, *Been in the Storm*, 414–15; Nashville *Republican Banner*, November 24, 1865; J. A. Fulton to Oliver O. Howard, October 11, 1865, Registered LR by the Asst. Commissioner for Ky. and Tenn., RG 105, NA; Cincinnati *Gazette*, August 3, 1865; Cartmell Diary, June–August 1865; Porter Diary, March–September 1865; Bills Diary, June–August 1865.

21. Lane, *Autobiography*, 57; John A. Henry to R. W. Barnard, August 7, 1865, Reports Relating to Freedmen's Homes and Hospitals, RG 105, NA; F. Ayer to M. E. Streiby, October 2, 1865, AMA; Nashville *Republican Banner*, October 6, 1865; Memphis *Argus*, August 23–25, 1865; Trowbridge, *The South*, 251.

22. Nashville *Gazette*, November 17, 1865; Gallatin *Examiner* ex-

cerpt in Nashville *Dispatch*, November 14, 1865; Daingen Rhodes et al. to Clinton B. Fisk, December 17, 1865, and J. H. Gregory to Clinton B. Fisk, November 8, 1865, Registered LR by the Asst. Commissioner for Ky. and Tenn., RG 105, NA; Law Court of Chattanooga, Civil Record A, pt. 2, 445, 476, typescript at TSLA.

23. John Seage to J. T. Alden, January 17, 1866, John W. Jones to Clinton B. Fisk, January 24, 1866, and "List of Outrages," Reports of Outrages filed with the Asst. Commissioner for Ky. and Tenn., RG 105, NA; William French to Clinton B. Fisk, September 14, 1865, and J. B. Mercer et al., "Proceedings of Union Depot Meeting," November 23, 1865, Registered LR by the Asst. Commissioner for Ky. and Tenn., RG 105, NA; William G. Rutledge to John A. Henry, September 1, 1865, Unregistered LR by the Knoxville Subassistant Commissioner, RG 105, NA.

24. Table 8 is based upon all existing bureau contract records for 1865 (Dyer, Gibson, Fayette, Franklin, Hardeman, Madison, Robertson, Shelby, Tipton, and Wilson counties). Tenn. Sheet Contracts and Tenn. vols. 102, 104, 214, RG 105, NA; Taylor, *Negro in Tennessee*, 150.

25. New York *Anglo-African*, November 29, 1865 (quoted); *U.S. Statutes at Large*, XIII, 508; W. L. Washington to Jane Washington, March 11, 1865, Mary Washington to George A. Washington, [1865], and Mary Washington to Jane Washington, March 5, 1865, Washington Papers; *AS*, supp. ser. 1, VII, 629; Memphis *Appeal*, November 18, 1865.

26. Clinton B. Fisk to Oliver O. Howard, July 27, August 27, 1865, Tenn. vol. 15, 17, 38, RG 105, NA; Gerteis, *Contraband*, 187–88; Smith, "Emancipation," 275–76.

27. Belz, *Emancipation*, 62–71; Gerteis, *Contraband*, 187.

28. Gerteis, *Contraband*, 188–91; Nashville *Press and Times*, October 18, 1865; Clinton B. Fisk to John M. Shultz, December 15, 1865, Tenn. vol. 7, 295, RG 105, NA; John Seage to Clinton B. Fisk, October 3, 1865, Registered LR by the Asst. Commissioner for Ky. and Tenn., RG 105, NA; *Freedmen's Bulletin*, II (December 1865), 8–9 (quoted).

29. *Pennsylvania Freedmen's Bulletin*, I (December 1865), 70, 73; Rose, *Rehearsal for Reconstruction*, 387–89; *Senate Executive Docu-*

ments, 39 Cong., 1 Sess., No. 27, 13; A. C. Swartzwelder to Clinton B. Fisk, December 18, 1865, Registered LR by the Asst. Commissioner for Ky. and Tenn., RG 105, NA.

30. Memphis *Argus,* May 14, 1865; Nashville *Dispatch,* May 30, 1865; James A. Rogers to William G. Brownlow, May 15, 1865, William G. Brownlow Gubernatorial Papers, TSLA; Alfred Bearden to J. G. Carrigan, October 23, 1865, Petitions to the 1865–67 General Assembly, TSLA; Tennessee, *House Journal,* 1865–67 General Assembly, 1 Sess., 133 (May 8, 1865), Adjourned Sess., 224 (December 5, 1865), 239–40 (December 12, 1865).

31. Knoxville Board of Mayor and Aldermen, Minute Book D., 297–98, City Archives, Knoxville; Nashville *Republican Banner,* November 1, 1865; Law Court of Chattanooga, Civil Record A, pt. 2, 460; John A. Henry to George Stoneman, December 5, 1865, Tenn. vol. 118, 111, RG 105, NA; Charles E. McDougall to R. W. Johnson, July 26, 1865, LR by the District of Middle Tennessee, RG 393, NA.

32. A. B. Lucas to John A. Cochrane, November 10, 1865, Unregistered LR by the Chattanooga Superintendent, RG 105, NA; Nashville *Dispatch,* December 14, 1865; James C. Babbitt to W. T. Clarke, October 23, 31, 1865, David Boyd to W. T. Clarke, October 5, 1865, and John M. Arnent to Clinton B. Fisk, July 27, 1865, Registered LR by the Asst. Commissioner for Ky. and Tenn., RG 105, NA; George Brown to William G. Brownlow, November 13, 1865, Brownlow Gubernatorial Papers; A. J. Fletcher to Jehu Baker, December 29, 1865, Brownlow/Baker Correspondence; Tennessee, *Senate Journal Appendix,* 1865–67 General Assembly, 1 Sess., 3d foldout sheet between 112–13.

33. Nashville *Press and Times,* July 24, 1865; *House Executive Documents,* 39 Cong., 1 Sess., No. 70, 46, 49; Taylor, *Negro in Tennessee,* 16–19.

34. Taylor, *Negro in Tennessee,* chap. 11; Matthews Diary, June 25, August 20, 1865; Records of the First Baptist Church of Nashville, vol. for 1860–73, 81, 88; S. G. Silliman et al. to N. A. M. Dudley, November 25, 1865, Registered LR by the Asst. Commissioner for Ky. and Tenn., RG 105, NA; W. W. Clayton, *History of Davidson County, Tennessee* (Philadelphia, 1880), 327, 333; New York *Anglo-African,* September 3, 1865.

35. Gutman, *Black Family*, 140–43; *House Executive Documents*, 39 Cong., 1 Sess., No. 70, 181; *AS*, XVIII, 50, XIX, 205, supp. ser. 1, V, 215, VIII, 1088, supp. ser. 2, IX, 3441; Case of Archer Thompson and Lizzie Merick, August 16, 1865, Tenn. vol. 170, 34, RG 105, NA; John Cochrane to S. B. F. C. Barr, October 20, 1865, Tenn. vol. 7, 128, RG 105, NA.

36. New York *Times*, October 8, 1865; Nashville *Press and Times*, September 19, October 12, 1865; Taylor, *Negro in Tennessee*, chap. 9.

37. J. E. Hillary Skinner, *After the Storm* (2 vols., London, 1866), I, 25; Nashville *Republican Banner*, October 18, 1865; Knoxville *Whig and Rebel Ventilator*, September 27, 1865; Nashville *Dispatch*, September 17, 1865; Trowbridge, *The South*, 239; Memphis *Argus*, September 26, 1865; C. W. Van Akin to Clinton B. Fisk, July 31, 1865, Registered LR by the Asst. Commissioner for Ky. and Tenn., RG 105, NA.

38. Anthony Carter to Clinton B. Fisk, October 12, 1865, and Jerry E. Galbraith to Clinton B. Fisk, October 5, 1865, Registered LR by the Asst. Commissioner for Ky. and Tenn., RG 105, NA; Memphis *Argus*, May 25, 1865; Jonesboro *East Tennessee Flag*, November 10, 1865; Nashville *Colored Tennessean*, August 12, 1865; Alexander, *Reconstruction in Tennessee*, 154–60.

39. Nashville *Times and Press*, May 27, September 2, 1865; Berlin, *Slaves without Masters*, 384; Nashville *Dispatch*, July 30, 1865; Tennessee, *Senate Journal*, 1865–67 General Assembly, 1 Sess., 22 (April 6, 1865); Marshall Wingfield, ed., "The Diary of Williamson Younger (1817–1876)," *West Tennessee Historical Society Papers* (1959), 70–71.

40. Nashville *Dispatch*, May 30, July 23, 1865; Memphis *Argus*, September 26, 1865; Bolivar *Bulletin* excerpt in Nashville *Union*, September 15, 1865; Fayetteville *Observer*, December 21, 1865; Anthony Carter to Clinton B. Fisk, October 12, 1865, and Joel B. Smith to Clinton B. Fisk, December 25, 1865, Registered LR by the Asst. Commissioner for Ky. and Tenn., RG 105, NA; Nashville *Dispatch*, July 23, 1865. Seven schools were set on fire in 1865, compared with three in 1862–64. See Joel B. Smith to Clinton B. Fisk, November 12, 1865, Registered LR by the Asst. Commissioner for Ky. and Tenn., RG 105, NA; Nashville *Press and Times*, September 9,

1865; E. M. Mears to John Ogden, October 14, 1865, S. P. Anderson to John Ogden, October 3, 1865, and R. J. Creswell to Clinton B. Fisk, December 12, 1865, AMA; "List of Outrages," Reports of Outrages filed with the Asst. Commissioner for Ky. and Tenn., RG 105, NA; and E. H. Van Tuyl to ?, September 12, 1865, LR by the District of Middle Tennessee, RG 393, NA.

41. Knoxville *Whig and Rebel Ventilator,* August 23, September 27, 1865; Cleveland *Banner,* October 21, 1865; Nashville *Dispatch,* November 12, December 2, 1865; Clarksville *Chronicle,* August 19, 1865.

42. Henry Corbin to Cinton B. Fisk, October 16, 1865, and William French to Clinton B. Fisk, September 8, 1865, Registered LR by the Asst. Commissioner for Ky. and Tenn., RG 105, NA; John E. Smith to A. J. Alexander, November 9, 1865, vol. 1–DWT, 175, RG 393, NA; "List of Outrages," Reports of Outrages filed with the Asst. Commissioner for Ky. and Tenn., RG 105, NA; Samuel Evans to N. A. M. Dudley, October 10, 1865, Unregistered LR by the Memphis Subassistant Commissioner, RG 105, NA.

43. *AS,* XVIII, 37, 118, 133 (quoted), 205, 295, 305, XIX, 217.

Bibliographical Essay

Prior to the 1930s historians wrote little about slavery during the Civil War. W. E. Burghardt Du Bois's *Black Reconstruction* (New York, 1935) included the first sympathetic overview of black wartime activities. Bell Irvin Wiley's subsequent *Southern Negroes, 1861–1865* (New Haven, 1938) supplied a wealth of data drawn from previously untapped sources. Benjamin Quarles, *The Negro in the Civil War* (Boston, 1953), eloquently surveyed the subject within a larger framework. These early studies established the assertiveness of contrabands and pointed to areas needing further investigation.

Major new interpretive forays appeared later in Eugene D. Genovese, *Roll, Jordan, Roll: The World the Slaves Made* (New York, 1974), Edward Magdol, *A Right to the Land: Essays on the Freedmen's Community* (Westport, Conn., 1977), Leon F. Litwack, *Been in the Storm So Long: The Aftermath of Slavery* (New York, 1979), and Paul D. Escott, *Slavery Remembered: A Record of Twentieth Century Slave Narratives* (Chapel Hill, N.C., 1979). Together, they cover the range of possible slave responses to the war.

The first monographic study of wartime slaves was Willie Lee Rose, *Rehearsal for Reconstruction: The Port Royal Experiment* (Indianapolis, 1964). Her superbly written account deals with the unique case of the South Carolina Sea Islands but contains an acute analysis of Northern reformers. C. Peter Ripley, *Slaves and Freedmen in Civil War Louisiana* (Baton Rouge, La., 1976), studies a larger, more typical area. His forte lies in determining factors behind federal policy decisions.

Bibliographical Essay

Little has been written on slavery's end in Tennessee. Neither Caleb Perry Patterson, *The Negro in Tennessee, 1790–1865* (Austin, Tex., 1922), nor Chase C. Mooney, *Slavery in Tennessee* (Bloomington, Ind., 1957), despite their titles, covers the war years. Bobby L. Lovett, "The Negro's Civil War in Tennessee," *Journal of Negro History*, LXI (January 1976), 36–50, and "The Negro in Tennessee: A Socio-Military History of the Civil War Era" (Ph.D. dissertation, University of Arkansas, 1978), deal with some aspects of the subject. Alrutheus Ambush Taylor, *The Negro in Tennessee, 1865–1880* (Washington, 1941), is a pioneering study of black Tennesseans after the war.

Several excellent primary sources illustrate how the war affected relations between masters and slaves in Tennessee. The L. Virginia French Diary (Tennessee State Library and Archives, Nashville, Tennessee) and the Harding-Jackson Papers (Southern Historical Collection, University of North Carolina Library, Chapel Hill, North Carolina) detail the relationships of masters with loyal slaves. Lucid, intensely personal accounts of slave disloyalty appear in the Robert H. Cartmell Diary and the Sarah Bailey Kennedy Papers at the Tennessee State Library and Archives, the John Houston Bills and Nimrod Porter diaries in the Southern Historical Collection, and Sarah Ridley Trimble, ed., "Behind the Lines in Middle Tennessee: The Journal of Bettie Ridley Blackmoor," *Tennessee Historical Quarterly*, XII (March 1953), 48–80.

A number of Tennessee slaves described their wartime experiences in George P. Rawick, ed., *The American Slave: A Composite Autobiography* (41 vols., Westport, Conn., 1972–79), a set of interviews conducted by the Works Progress Administration and Fisk University during the 1930s. Users must keep in mind that interviewees spontaneously verbalized their memories in a folksy and idiomatic style, which should not be read as literally as a memoir deliberately written for publication. The speakers tended to trust black interviewers more; for this reason, the Fisk volumes include most of the more revealing narratives. A valuable supplement to the Rawick collection is Orland Kay Armstrong, *Old Massa's People: The Old Slaves Tell Their Story* (Indianapolis, 1931). George L. Knox, *Slave and Freeman*, ed. by Willard B. Gatewood, Jr. (Lexington, Ky., 1979), ranks as the most revealing of the few Tennessee slave autobiographies that touch on the war years.

No highly useful secondary or primary sources exist on Confederate policies toward slaves. Even the National Archives' Confederate Records contain disappointingly little. Pertinent material from both sides of the war appears in U.S. War Department, *The War of the Rebellion: A Compilation of the Official Records of the Union and Confederate Armies* (131 vols., Washington, 1880–1901).

Materials about federal policies toward slaves abound. The major study is Louis S. Gerteis, *From Contraband to Freedman: Federal Policy toward Southern Blacks, 1861–1865* (Westport, Conn., 1973), which perceptively analyzes economic programs but pays insufficient attention to social programs. In the National Archives, the Records of the United States Army Continental Commands, 1821–1920, offer a wealth of data from all levels of the military occupation's hierarchy and from directors of black recruitment. Adjutant General Lorenzo Thomas's central role in directing contraband programs in the Mississippi Valley makes the Records of the Office of the Adjutant General important. They include not only his official papers but also those of the American Freedmen's Inquiry Commission, black regiments, and General William T. Sherman. Records of the Bureau of Refugees, Freedmen, and Abandoned Lands provide a few documents about wartime contraband programs and many about postwar race relations.

John Eaton, *Grant, Lincoln, and the Freedmen* (New York, 1907), details the evolution of contraband policy in West Tennessee and his leading role in it. His Freedmen's Department published a number of reports as pamphlets, the most informative being John Eaton, *Report of the General Superintendent of Freedmen, Department of the Tennessee and State of Arkansas for 1864* (Memphis, 1865), and Joseph Warren, ed., *Extracts from Reports of Superintendents of Freedmen* (Vicksburg, Miss., 1864).

Dudley Taylor Cornish, *The Sable Arm: Negro Troops in the Union Army, 1861–1865* (New York, 1956), ably surveys another important aspect of the army's relationship with blacks. Robert Cowden, *A Brief Sketch of the Organization and Services of the Fifty-Ninth Regiment of United States Colored Infantry* (Dayton, Ohio, 1885), Thomas J.

Bibliographical Essay

Morgan, *Reminiscences of Service with Colored Troops in the Army of the Cumberland, 1863–1865* (Providence, R. I., 1885), Henry Romeyn, *With Colored Troops in the Army of the Cumberland* (n.p., 1904), and Ira Berlin, ed., *Freedom: A Documentary History of Emancipation, 1861–1867* (1 vol. to date, New York, 1982–), offer insight into black military service.

Records of Northern civilian reformers, mostly in the form of letters to freedmen's aid societies, are not so plentiful as the military materials. Correspondence files of only one of the societies active in Tennessee have survived: the American Missionary Association Archives, in the Amistad Research Center, Dillard University, New Orleans. The archives contain all letters published in the association's journal, *American Missionary*, and much more. Correspondence of other societies can be found only in their journals or reports. The most useful journals were *Freedmen's Bulletin* of the Northwestern Freedmen's Aid Commission, *Freedmen's Friend* of the Association of Friends for the Aid and Elevation of the Freedmen, *Home Evangelist* of the American Baptist Home Mission Society, and *Pennsylvania Freedmen's Bulletin* of the Pennsylvania Freedmen's Relief Association.

Reformers left only a few lengthy accounts of their work. Frank R. Levstik, ed., "A Journey among the Contrabands: The Diary of Walter Totten Carpenter," *Indiana Magazine of History*, LXXIII (September 1977), 204–22, and *Senate Executive Documents*, 38th Congress, 1st Session, Number 28, record two inspections of contraband living conditions by observant Northern philanthropists. Elvira J. Powers, *Hospital Pencilings* (Boston, 1866), pays much attention to the activities and attitudes of the contrabands. R. W. McGranahan, ed., *Historical Sketch of the Freedmen's Missions of the United Presbyterian Church, 1862–1904* (Knoxville, 1904), contains both primary and secondary accounts of that denomination's projects in Tennessee.

The best narrative of wartime politics in Tennessee, despite some factual errors, remains Clifton R. Hall, *Andrew Johnson: Military Governor of Tennessee* (Princeton, N.J., 1916). Peter Maslowski, *Treason Must Be Made Odious: Military Occupation and Wartime Reconstruction in Nashville, Tennessee, 1862–1865* (Millwood, N.Y.,

184

1978), though not so detailed or broad, is more reliable. Major sources for political information are the David Campbell Papers (Duke University Library, Durham, North Carolina) and the Andrew Johnson Papers (Library of Congress); a number of the latter have been annotated in LeRoy P. Graf and Ralph W. Haskins, eds., *The Papers of Andrew Johnson* (6 vols. to date, Knoxville, 1967–).

Wartime newspapers stressed politics but included information on every aspect of slavery's deterioration. Besides news stories and editorials, useful information shows up in advertising columns, court reports, municipal government reports, and official notices. The only national papers that frequently printed Tennessee news were the Chicago *Tribune* and the Cincinnati *Gazette*, radical Republican organs. Wartime papers in Tennessee were few, yet varied in political outlook. The Nashville *Union* grew progressively radical until Samuel C. Mercer lost the editorship in late 1863. It remained affiliated with the Union party through 1865, but followed erratic editorial policies. In early 1864 Mercer founded the unabashedly radical Nashville *Times and True Union,* which constantly clashed with the Conservatives' Nashville *Press.* In May 1865 Mercer's financial backers deviously bought control of the *Press* and merged the two papers into the Nashville *Press and Times* under his editorship. The Nashville *Dispatch* officially held a neutral position during the war, but demonstrated Conservative leanings, which clearly came to the fore in 1865. The Memphis *Bulletin* had proslavery unionist editors after federal occupation until the antislavery James B. Bingham bought it in early 1863. Its Conservative opponent was the Memphis *Argus.* In East Tennessee William G. Brownlow's Knoxville *Whig and Rebel Ventilator* was so popular and vituperative that Conservatives did not print a competitor during the war.

Only the most important sources have been discussed here; other materials cited in the notes contribute bits of data or interpretive thought. The study of nineteenth-century American race relations requires collecting and piecing together numerous fragments of information, sometimes with disappointingly incomplete results. Such is the case with that part of a nation's past that the majority at the time did not care to remember.

Index

Index

Index

occupation of Tennessee, 3–5, 17–18, 20–22, 24, 27–28, 30, 32, 34, 38, 45–46, 62, 72, 146 (n. 20); campaigns, 16, 19, 27–29, 92–97; depredations, 19–20, 189; impact on slavery, 20–21, 31, 118–21; fugitive slave policies, 34–40, 48, 50, 60, 99, 144 (nn. 5, 9); military courts, 44–45, 123, 147 (n. 35); subsistence of contrabands, 48–59; use of black laborers, 65–66; demobilization, 124, 130. *See also* Soldiers

Fessenden, William P., 58
Fisk, Clinton B., 127
Fiske, Asa S., 61, 64, 74–75
Forrest, Nathan B., 92, 95–96
Fort Donelson, 14, 16, 34–35, 38, 50–51, 53, 61, 65, 81, 83
Fort Henry, 14, 16, 34
Fort Pillow, 14, 16, 49, 53, 92–96
Free blacks, 7, 16, 130; interaction with contrabands, 4, 47, 60, 76–77; laws governing, 44–45, 125, 127–28
Freedmen, 122, 131; status, 5, 123, 128–29; legal issues, 103, 115, 118, 127–28; labor issues, 121, 124–25, 127; hostility toward, 124–25, 127–28, 130–31; desire for land, 125–27; behavior, 129–30. *See also* Education, Family, Religion
Freedmen's aid societies, 54–57, 59–60, 76–78, 127
Freedmen's Bureau, 120, 124–29
Freedmen's Departments, 49–52, 54, 59–60, 63, 67, 74–75, 127, 129
Fugitive Slave Act of 1850, 37, 99

Gallatin, 50, 51, 53, 55, 58, 67, 70, 76, 83, 90, 113
Georgia, 96
Ghettos, black, 46–48, 57
Gibson County, Tennessee, 120
Grant, Ulysses S., 34, 37, 48–49, 51, 57, 65, 82, 85–86

Hadley, Ben J., 111
Hall, C. R., 122
Halleck, Henry, 34–37
Hardeman County, Tennessee, 13
Harding, Henry, 111
Harding, William G., 20
Harris, Ransom, 110
Hawkins County, Tennessee, 13
Haywood County, Tennessee, 22, 120–21
Helena, Arkansas, 49
Helper, Hinton Rowan, 107
Henderson, Morris, 75, 110–11
Hickman, Wade, 44–45, 110–11
Hickman County, Tennessee, 30, 120
Hood, James R., 115
Hood, John B., 51–52, 66, 96–97
Hubbard, William C., 77–78
Humphrey, Lucinda, 76, 78–79
Hunt, Ralph, 51, 68
Huntsville, Tennessee, 122

Island No. 10, 16, 49, 53, 55–56, 58

Jackson, Tennessee, 13, 49, 53, 82
Johnson, Andrew, 66, 86; unionist leader, 12, 33–34, 98, 102; antislavery actions, 43–45, 103–10, 114–16; views, 50, 82–83, 113–15; proslavery actions, 98–102; president, 119, 123, 126
Johnson, Ebenezer, 29
Johnsonville, Tennessee, 89, 96
Jordan, William, 44, 76

Kennedy, Sarah, 28
Kentucky, 86, 102
Killebrew, Joseph B., 27
Kimball, Nathan, 82
Knox, George, 24, 59
Knoxville, Tennessee, 17, 52, 54, 76–77, 83, 109, 111, 128

La Grange, Tennessee, 49, 53, 56, 58, 82, 122
Lapsly, Daniel, 111

188

Index

Index

Proslavery Theory, 9–10, 13, 26–27, 32, 41, 61, 71, 119, 130
Pulaski, Tennessee, 38, 50–57, 64, 70, 76, 79, 83, 96

Randolph, David, 111
Rankin, Horatio N., 110–11
Reconstruction: general, 60–62, 119, 123, 127, 131; economic, 62–72; social, 72–80; political, 102, 105, 114–17
Reformers, 4, 47–48, 58–59, 128–30; laissez-faire group, 61–62, 64, 69, 85–86, 127; paternalistic group, 61–62, 69, 71–75, 82, 127
Religion: for slaves, 11, 21–22, 29, 135 (n. 10); for contrabands, 47, 72–73, 76, 80, 85; for freedmen, 129–30
Republican party, 6, 16, 34, 36, 83, 98–99, 106, 108. *See also* Union party
Ridley, Rebecca, 23, 25
Rosecrans, William S., 37–38, 65, 82–83
Rousseau, Lovell H., 39–40, 44, 66, 68, 86, 89
Rutherford County, Tennessee, 23

Scaggs, David, 111
Scott, George, 112
Scurlock, John C., 111
Secessionists, 12, 101, 105, 116; views, 6–7, 10, 13, 108; punished, 17, 24, 34, 37, 40; hostility toward, 33, 36, 99, 117
Shane, William, 43
Shelby County, Tennessee, 27, 30, 41
Shelbyville, Tennessee, 83
Sherman, William T., 41–42, 52, 57, 85, 87, 92
Slave code, 10–11, 36–45, 81, 147 (n. 33)
Slavery: paternalism in, 3–4, 14, 19–20, 25, 29, 31, 122, 125; social aspects, 5, 7, 11–12, 128; economic aspects, 7, 123–24, 142 (n. 35); as an institution, 10–11, 17–19, 25, 27, 30, 34, 37, 60–61, 72, 81, 99, 106, 116, 120, 122–24, 131. *See also* Emancipation

Slaves: loyal, 4, 14, 20–21, 121, 143 (n. 43); disloyal, 4, 19–20, 22–32, 99; violence, 5, 6, 10, 12–13, 26, 85, 92, 94, 96; compensation, 7, 25, 27; sales, 10–11, 15, 17, 29; punishment, 10–11, 24, 30, 87, 120; visionaries, 20–22, 31; pragmatists, 20, 22, 31; abandoned, 27, 46, 71, 125; children, 29, 31, 120. *See also* Education, Family, Religion
Slaves (by first name): Aleck, 22; Betty, 27–28; Cherry, 25; Easter, 23; Granville, 16; Henry, 29; Henry, 122; Isaac, 6; Joel, 25; John, 25; Nancy, 21; Susanna, 20; Wiley, 29; William, 46
Smith, Abraham, 110, 112
Soldiers, black: enlistment, 31, 43, 81–88, 163 (nn. 13, 15), 165 (n. 26); families, 73–74, 84, 87, 89; views, 84, 90, 122; training, 88–89; views about, 91–92, 115, 118; noncombat duty, 91–92; combat duty, 92–97
Soldiers, white: Confederates, 22, 36, 92–95; Federals, 19, 21, 24–28, 30–31, 35–36, 38–40, 48–49, 55, 57, 65, 81, 86, 94–95, 110
South Carolina, 5, 28
Springfield, Tennessee, 76, 86
Stanton, Edwin M., 39, 57–58, 68, 81–83
Stearns, George L., 61, 62, 65–66, 82–85, 103
Stevenson, Alabama, 50–51
Stockwell, Elisha, 36
Stothart, Jerry, 112
Sumner, George, 112
Sumner, James, 112
Sumner, W. Alex, 112
Sumner, William, 110, 112
Surgeon general, U.S., 58
Swayne, John T., 41–42

Tate, Andrew, 110, 112
Tennessee constitution, 105–07, 115–16, 119, 123

190

ABOUT THE AUTHOR

John Cimprich teaches history at Southeast Missouri State University. He received his bachelor of arts degree from Thomas More College and his master of arts degree and his doctorate from Ohio State University. This is his first book.